TALKS FOR WOMEN'S MEETINGS

Talks For
Women's Meetings

FRANK CUMBERS

LONDON
EPWORTH PRESS

First published in 1967
by the Epworth Press

Book Steward
Frank H. Cumbers

Printed in Great Britain by
Billing & Sons Limited, Guildford and London

Contents

Acknowledgement

The New English Bible is copyright Oxford and Cambridge Presses 1961 and quotations from it are by kind permission.

1. *Done Your Packing?*

MORE people go away for holidays now than ever in the world before. One of our newspapers had a long article some years ago about Butlin's Camps, which Mr Billy Butlin (as he was then) reprinted and sent to a lot of people. 'If there were no Butlin's Camps,' said the article, 'someone would have had to invent them' . . . to meet the situation when perhaps millions more people were getting holidays with pay, than ever before. It would startle younger people to know what things were like, even before the Second War, about holidays. But there are few people who do not take them now.

Young people get priceless opportunities through their schools to see other lands and their people, before they are in their teens. You could really point to the travelling case, the valise, the hold-all, as the symbol of our times. Indeed, that was what someone said when John R. Mott retired. This famous American had spent years ceaselessly visiting land after land, making friends everywhere, and trying to link all these friends together. 'A picture of John R. Mott with a travelling case in one hand would stand very well for a symbol of Christian unity!' said one of his friends.

Luggage, then, becomes important. Parents travelling with two or three lively children know that they will need a lot of things for the journey—eatables and drinkables, crayons and nursery rhymes and fairy tales, and small games of every sort. Some of our ministers who go about preaching know to a millimetre where things go in the case which they pack nearly every Friday or Saturday of their lives!

What are *you* like at packing? It's a science—or can be!—

and there is more in it than just ramming a few things into
the bag about five minutes before the absolute zero hour
for your train or plane.

First of all, your case has only a certain amount of
room. 'First of all' is perhaps not the right expression.
This fact is generally forced upon you a good deal later,
when the case is already crammed and all sorts of 'absolutely necessary' things still lie on the bed or the table.
Even if you own an 'expanding' case, for which the makers
may claim so much, the point still arrives when nothing
more will go in!

Packing is a bit like life; for there are certainly limits to
what we can get into *that*; and 'soon or late', too, the fact
of death must be reckoned with. 'Seventy years is your
ration!' says the Psalmist; 'you *may* manage eighty or a
bit more, but it's all over pretty soon!' (Ps. 90:10 —
without agreeing to all that the verse says!) There is no
need to call this 'gloomy talk': it is just a fact that must
be recognized.

For packing, as for life, it soon becomes clear—we
can't get everything in; so we shall have to choose! One
of the classics on this subject is the famous book, *Three
Men in a Boat*, by Jerome K. Jerome, over which genera-
tions of readers have chuckled. You may remember that
they decided to take their boat up the Thames, and they
started by making a list of the things that they would
need for the journey.

Trouble soon arose. 'It was clear that the upper
reaches of the Thames would not allow of the navigation
of a boat sufficiently large for the things we had set down
as indispensable, so we tore up the list and looked at one
another. George said, "You know, we're on the wrong
tack altogether. We must not think of the things we
could do with, but only of the things we can't do
without!" '

Sensible advice. George speaks for all wise people, both in packing and in life.

Second: when packing—start in good time. Some people really start packing from the moment they end their previous journey! They leave in the case things that they'll need next time, but won't want until then; and from that time onwards they will put other things in the case as and when they can be spared. This is perhaps a bit excessive—but it's a good idea to start with time to spare. It's dangerous to rely on getting a few quiet and tranquil minutes for the packing just before you leave. There are some people who seem to find a thrill in this last-minute rush; they stumble into the carriage when the train is on the move, and smile triumphantly, even while they pant for their next breath. But it's much more sensible to give yourself time. Life is much the same. You can read wonderful stories of 'death-bed conversions' to Christianity in the last moments of life—and all this can be very real. What a wonderful thing! Yet isn't there something more wonderful in what Count Zinzendorf told the enquiring John Wesley—that he had known and enjoyed the love of God since he was two? The last-minute rush is all right, but the other makes for better packing, and for happier living.

We were thinking about those 'three men' in their boat. They discovered something else about packing, when they got down to it. All three, together with Montmorency, the dog, set to work very hard, but things didn't go very well. '. . . Harris packed the strawberry jam on a tomato, and squashed it, and they had to pick out the tomato with a teaspoon. They packed the pies at the bottom and put heavy things on top and smashed the pies in . . .'

Get the big things at the bottom! Some of these 'parables' don't need much interpreting, do they? When you go shopping you keep this rule if you are wise, and your

electric light bulbs will arrive home safely. Life is much
the same. A man said once, 'I defy anybody to read, or to
say to himself, every morning or night, St Paul's thirteenth
chapter of First Corinthians, without it making a real
difference to everything he does!' That could be true—
and if a man thinks about God as He has revealed Himself
in Jesus, he is bound to be a different man—a better man—
in every moment of the day: at home, at work, on the
sports field, at the concert hall, or wherever. *Get the big
things in at the start—at the bottom.*

It is very instructive to watch a real master-packer.
Every bit of space is used; nothing with any kind of hole
in it is allowed to escape; socks (of course) are tucked
into shoes, and any pot or box packed full with small
things. If a careful mother packs for her son when he goes
on holiday, things can be a bit difficult for him on the
return journey when he comes to re-pack in order to go
home. He is likely to have a bulging case long before the
pile around him has disappeared, and he gasps, 'How on
earth did *she* get it all in?' We feel the same amazement
when we think of the lives of truly great men and women.
They direct large undertakings; they deal with perhaps
hundreds or thousands of people; their interests are
widespread—but they still have room for the small and
imaginative kindly act that 'makes the day' for someone
else. It was at a time when Jesus was weighing up heavier
problems than any man had ever known that He had
leisure of mind to notice and to praise the widow who
timidly slipped her two tiny coins into the offering-box.
At that same time He gave their health and strength to
many who were weak and sad. Use life to the full, like the
great ones. It's *love* that makes it possible, not so much
wisdom or cleverness. Get in everything you can, un-
hurriedly, steadily, methodically. Be it items to pack or a
day to live, look around you, think, and plan.

What sort of packer are you? You realize the answer to that soon enough—for the proof of the packing is . . . the unpacking! You may have packed swiftly or slowly, methodically or haphazardly, but . . . how do the things come out of the case? It is then that a packer knows that he 'needs not to be ashamed'—or the reverse! It cannot be claimed that all slow packers are good packers, or that all who do the job swiftly land in trouble; sometimes it is quite the other way round! This, too, is a question for life as much as for travelling. At every stage the Parable of the Talents (Matthew 25) has the refrain 'Well done, good and faithful servant . . .' or the reverse. When life is ended and you meet His gaze, it will be good to have lived so as to gain His 'Well done!'

Just one more word. When you've packed your case it may well be heavy. You've kept all the rules that we have remembered here, but—there's no doubt about it—you've got a load to carry. Well, then—so long as you are sound in wind and limb—step it out with a swinging stride and make light of the journey, if not of the case! This may sound a bit hard—but you will find it very much harder if you lift your case limply and walk slowly and painfully. The journey then will seem a hundred times longer. If you start off with a good will, stepping it out, you will have done a lot of your journey with your *first* wind—and the *second* wind will soon follow. 'Let him take up his cross . . .' said Jesus. (Another question: Is there a special point in that word 'his'?—has everyone a cross? And if so—who is carrying mine, if I'm not?)

In this difficult day, there is a special blessing awaiting the cheerful traveller—'A merry heart goes all the way; The sad tires in a mile-a!' And since, grimly enough, the 'sad heart' still has the other miles to face anyway, the sad heart faces a double burden. So, if you can . . . but why talk of what *you* can do, when, for the Christian, it is what 'God and I' can do that is the question? God loves to help us carry our burdens. The Christian is a *realist*, not an optimist. If he faces a stiff climb, he doesn't pretend that it is a relaxing stroll. But he remembers his Friend, and he is not dismayed.

2. *The Finishing Touch*

On the top of the pillars was lilywork: so was the
work of the pillars finished. (1 *Kings* 7: 22.)

'LILYWORK'! It's a lovely sounding word, and most
attractive. Actually the learned men are not sure what
some of these words mean in this story of the Temple
building. It is no wonder, perhaps, if words written so
long ago—and, for all we know, technical words used by
Hebrew craftsmen—are a bit difficult for us to understand
today. We are not very sure, then, what the lilywork was
like; but it certainly sounds very nice!

Now here is a question: 'Which was more important—
the pillars or the lilywork?' 'Why,' you say, 'the pillars,
of course! They supported everything; the lilywork
(whatever it was) was just the trimmings. Very nice, of
course, but . . .' and then perhaps you stop, for you
remember what this building was. It was a temple; it was
there for one thing—to make people think about God, and
to adore His ways. Our great churches and cathedrals,
and the small churches with their square towers or their
steeples, with a few houses nestling around them, these
do lift our thoughts to God. You can sometimes see the
towers of a cathedral miles away across the fields, as you
come in from the country—you may think of Peterborough
Cathedral as it shows for miles across the level Fens, or
of little Wells through some Mendip gap. Then there is
the might of Durham, seen high on its towering cliff, and
Salisbury . . . but we shall never get on with our question
in this way—and yet perhaps we shall. If the Temple was
raised to lift men's hearts nearer to God, it needed something more than the dull stubborn strength that merely
kept it standing.

When the students at Richmond College used to ask their theological Professor, Dr Ryder Smith, what they fondly thought was a 'poser' of a question, he would stroke his famous moustache reflectively, and then say, 'The answer to your question, Mr . . . , is "yes" . . . and . . . "no" !' No one ever got much change out of *him*! And you may have suspected that this is going to be much the same. Let us think further about this question, and take our choice.

We started by thinking of a building; but perhaps we see the point better in *people*. Really successful living will have both strength *and* beauty. There are some strong characters—with no beauty. Unfortunately, the people we call 'good' are always in danger of this. It was Hetty Wesley, tragic sister of John and Charles, who said one day to their father amid her tears, 'Sir—you are a good man; but you are seldom kind!' Even she in that moment did not deny his goodness; and no one does today, especially now that a reaction has set in, in his favour; for there were times when the amazing greatness of his wife Susanna tended to overshadow Samuel Wesley, sometimes rather unfairly. Arnold Bennett's parents were like that, we are told; and even if we suspect that we have only one side of *that* story, it gives us something to think about. Arnold Bennett might not have criticized Methodism so much in his stories if his parents had made him happier.

John the Baptist seems to have been a man of this sort. For John, things were black or white; there was no middle way. Perhaps John's life could have ended in no other way—though the evil woman who engineered his death gained nothing in the long run. Paul is at the opposite extreme from John the Baptist; for (it could surprise some readers to know) this little man could be very understanding, tactful, and kind. He could be firm, but his letter to Philemon shows how attractive he could be.

We must not despise the Samuel Wesleys, the John Baptists. They are strong; they are pillars, and the established ways of life might well shift and move if these did not stand so foursquare and courageous. Life is not easy for them; remember how John the Baptist died— and they do not take their stand for gain, but to satisfy strong convictions and ideals. You can *depend* upon them. They certainly teach us a lesson, in their strength and their sacrifice. But . . . they are not always very attractive. Consciously or unconsciously, they are *narrow*. If you told them that they were narrow, you might not disturb them; they might even take a pride in it. They rejoice in the strength; they may even suspect that if they once let doubt of any kind into their system, it would weaken the whole structure. But there must be strain and effort in it; and strain is never beautiful.

Have you ever noticed that, almost invariably, the best way to do a thing turns out to be the graceful, the beautiful way? Have you seen a man using a scythe? There is scything and scything, as you may know! Watch the golfer's swing, the footballer's pass to the centre, the movements of the ballet dancer, the rhythm of the blacksmith's stroke, the motions of the girl packing chocolates in their box. . . . The time and motion people know this, and they seek to guide people into economy of effort, and effectiveness. You may have read books by Robert Louis Stevenson, and you will have noticed his easy, unforced English—or, rather, you probably haven't noticed it at all, because it *is* so easy. But . . . take a pen and try to do it yourself! Not one writer in ten thousand can approach it. It's so easy! But it seems so because it is so right. Stevenson had *arrived*. Kathleen Ferrier's singing, in several languages, had that same 'easy' perfection. But read her life, and of her struggles to pronounce the 'r' and the 'l', and to give French and German vowels their proper sound!

Jesus our Lord was 'good *and* gay', and this is what attracts. There are some people, the very sight of whom does you good. They are obviously enjoying life; they have *zest*. Not that they 'have it easy', but they seem to get by their difficulties in such a way that you may not realize that they have them; it is very easy to overlook other people's troubles! But things live when they are about. You can hardly analyse what it is that happens; they are often not specially brainy or outstanding people. They are just alive; gloriously alive; and it makes life for others.

Strength without beauty? It's sad to see so much solid worth so little loved, and with so little entry into other people's hearts. These people are respected, but not loved. Sadly, they can get in the way of the cause which they have most at heart. There is a truly comic history-book, *1066 And All That*, which speaks shrewdly, if a bit sweepingly, about the Cavaliers, who were 'wrong but romantic', and the Roundheads, 'right but repulsive'!

But there is the opposite danger—beauty without strength. We all know people like that—they are charming and attractive. They are delightful pagans. Everyone here will know such people—gay, inconsequent, happy-go-lucky. And everyone may have thought at times that some of these people are a lot nicer than some church people we know! They make the dull 'Puritan' types look stuffy—so long as everything goes well for them. They know the lovely things of life, they rejoice in good music, fine poetry and the like . . . but there is a flaw. They do not grapple with life's hard facts.

The famous psychologist, Sigmund Freud, spoke of 'the reality principle'—it is perhaps no accident that he lived and worked in the 'gay city' of Vienna. You can think of the lovely lilting measure of Johann Strauss's waltz music —how gay and confident! But in that same city the patient psychologist found, hidden beneath the gaiety, some stark tragedies.

These people are wonderful for the trimmings—the decor of the theatre, the flags for the bridge, the gracious patterns in the garden—once someone of tougher (and maybe less attractive) breed has toiled to dig the theatre's foundations, to defy the river's flood with the deep supports which carry the bridge, to sweat and toil in the clay, and weed and clip away! They have charm, but they cannot grapple; they have no root.

So we are coming to see that the answer to our question is that we need both—the strength and the lilywork. True success in life depends upon both together—strength and beauty; dependability *and* attractiveness. How good it is to remember that the Christian has a word which expresses the two of them together—the word *Grace*. Grace is a lovely word; the most beautiful word in the Christian vocabulary. Grace *is* strength plus beauty.

There is striving in life.

Our England is a garden, and such gardens are not made
By saying, 'O how beautiful', and sitting in the shade.

Christ was gay, as we have seen. But Christ prayed, and prayed long until, in the Scripture word, he sweated blood, 'with strong crying and tears'. We need both strength and beauty; just as the Temple needed the powerful pillars for upholding, *and* the lilywork that all might be 'glorious within', and that it might lead men's souls to God. My aim, my vision, must be this grace; this joining together of unflinching strength and of breathless beauty—the strength and the beauty of the God who made mighty constellations, and tiny rills

B

bubbling between the rocks. The Christian who is guided by his Lord has the strength to storm the frowning gates of hell; and he has the love and humbleness to turn in the moment of his victory to wash the feet of a brother. Here is the good news; we can reach this somewhere, sometime, in this world or the next, if we make it our business to follow Jesus.

3. *Where Your Treasure is . . . and Where is it?*

Do YOU know the party game where the man in charge says abruptly, 'Bread!' and you have to answer with the first word that comes to your mind? In that instance, most people would answer, 'Butter', perhaps. Though, until not very long ago, if someone had answered, 'Margarine', the other people would have drawn certain conclusions! Nowadays, of course, margarine is very, very much improved. It looks easy enough, doesn't it? 'Boy'— 'Girl'; 'Horse!' . . . well, 'Cart' for most of us. But if a man playing this game goes to the races, he might react with 'Jockey' or 'Bet'; and we should know something about *him*! 'Cat' would lead many of us to say 'Milk!', but if a boy of one type is playing, he might gleefully say, 'Stone!' or 'Brick!', thus revealing his unfortunate reaction when a cat appears on the horizon! (His father might, of course, be a gardener, and we know that some gardeners have strong views about cats.)

Actually, of course, this game is the offshoot of something that matters quite a lot. Psychologists are very fond of using what they call 'free association', which is just this game turned to more realistic purposes, and are very often able to get a lot of information. 'Oh, but,' you say, 'I've often thought that when some people are playing the St Paul's game (or whatever you call it in your parts) they don't always *say* the first word they *think* of—it might be too revealing!' And there you are absolutely right. Some people do act like that, and certainly a murderer would, if he were being examined. But the psychologists are up to that one. If they were dealing with a suspected murderer, they would start on their 'free association' method, using quite innocent words, which could give nothing away. But then they would suddenly introduce a 'loaded' word. The man being questioned would think of the word which naturally 'answered' to that one, but would then think, 'I mustn't say *that*: it'll give the game away!', and he would quickly substitute another, less incriminating word instead! In answer to the word 'rope' he might well have the word 'strangle' or 'window' ready, but (after he had quickly thought) he might say, 'Tug-o'-war'. But he would have hesitated, flickered, just an instant before producing the substitute word, and the investigators would be timing him to the thousandth of a minute. And if they were able afterwards to sift through a list of (say) fifty words, including perhaps twenty that were 'loaded': and in each 'loaded' case they had recorded some very slight hesitation or delay in answering, they might feel justified in believing that this man knew something about the crime; he had had to hedge and fence in order to save himself from admitting something that might be dangerous!

So perhaps we may all think it best to be very careful the next time we play this game. We may give something away!

There is a text that says, 'As a man thinketh in his heart, so is he' (Prov. 23: 7). There is another text, too, upon which our title to this talk is based: a word of our Lord's, penetrating and challenging—'Where your treasure is, there will your heart be also' (Matt. 6: 21).

Our thoughts are like homing pigeons, and sooner or later will lead us back to some familiar thing. Dr Sangster had a vivid story in one of his great books.[1] In a German town, a woman found a basket on her doorstep, with a pigeon inside it *and* a note which threatened something very drastic if she did not fasten a certain sum of money to the clip on the pigeon's leg and then set the bird flying

[1] *Why Jesus Never Wrote a Book*, pp. 28-9.

again. She very wisely told the police immediately. The police chartered a plane and then, having released the bird, followed it and dropped a message to other policemen when they saw the place the bird went to. Those policemen questioned the men who were there, but they protested that the bird was not theirs. It had merely flown into that loft by accident. So the police took the bird away, and several times launched it into the air—and every time the bird flew to that very place!

Our ruling passions and interests always reveal themselves. A man who was taken around Wells Cathedral in Somerset listened with great attention to the guide's story. The guide was pleased to have so attentive a client, and he pointed to the wonderful inverted arches, the intricate carvings of the choir, and took him into the chapter house, supported by its single pillar. The guide really spread himself, but as they took a final view of the cathedral, the man looked around him and said, 'Aye—there's a tidy lot o' timber here!' He was a timber merchant on a very large scale; and the guide realized that when he thought he had him spellbound by the majesty of that holy place, the visitor was mentally measuring it all up, and probably working out the costs on present-day timber prices!

There was a young man who took his girl friend to a football match. She knew nothing about football, and he did his best to explain the rules, and to expound the finer points of the game. She listened with every appearance of interest, and he felt more and more sure that she was the girl for him. But suddenly there was a brilliant piece of play and a wonderful goal (for the home side, of course!). He turned to the girl at his side and said rapturously, 'What did you think of *that*?' She hesitated, even blushed a little, and then said, 'Well, I didn't actually see what happened . . . Did you ever see an uglier hat than that girl is wearing over there?' The young man

realized, of course, that so frivolous a girl was no true
helpmeet for a right-thinking man! And this was the last
time he took her out!

It is the same with everything we do. Our ruling passion
colours our interests, our attention, and our effort. Those
two words will bear a lot of pondering. What is *my* ruling
passion? Other people could tell me—if I have not
realized myself. My Lord could tell me.

Some people's thoughts always fly to Jesus. When some
difficulty arises, their first thought is, 'Lord, what do we
do now?' ('We', you notice. That is how the real Christian
lives. 'I live, yet not I, but Christ dwelleth in me'—
Gal. 2: 20.) He has helped them wonderfully so far, and
things will not change now.

> *His love in times past forbids me to think*
> *He'll leave me at last in trouble to sink.*

Joy and happiness are greater when shared with Him.
What a way to live; your sorrows shared, effort lifted
from your heart, joys redoubled and linked with the great
Power behind his wonderful universe! It sounds worth
reaching: how do we get there?

Well, it never happens by accident, nor (on the other
hand) is it achieved by determination. It happens as more
and more we bring ourselves to Him, but with such a
prize it is worth practising . . . the very word. One of the
world's most famous books on this subject is called *The
Practice of the Presence of God*.

Sometimes you will find articles in the newspapers and
magazines: 'How I play Tennis'. Miss This or Senorita
That will write an article on 'How to Follow Through';
or Mr So-and-So or some brilliant French player will
reveal the secrets of his success . . . And people wanting
to play like that will cut these articles from the paper, and
try and try to follow the advice. It's often very good

advice, but there is something missing. Sometimes when Miss So-and-so tries to explain just *how* she does it, she is not telling the whole story. She can't: she doesn't really know. It's a knack, as we say, and there are ever so many reactions, of body and mind, which produce the splendid result—for her! Not for other people; not, at least, in the five minutes which is all that most folk are prepared to give. So some are champions—and some are not!

When a man plays a game so expertly that he can do just what he wants with his bat, racquet, or whatever, *he has arrived*. But this comes only when time and time again he has tried, and often failed. He has known what he wanted to do; sometimes the thing would happen, and happen brilliantly. But he wasn't satisfied, because he didn't quite know how or why he had done it! He was never satisfied until he could rely on doing what he aimed at—more often than not, anyway.

It is the same for the man whose aim is to know his God. He *longs* to know Him, to live with Him. From that longing and that vision he persists in his aim, only because he realizes how wonderful it would be to succeed. It is wonderful for him now, but he got there only through discipline, months and years of it—calling himself back to his purpose when his mind strayed off to other things. It *is* so difficult to keep your thoughts steady on any particular thing. The psychologists say that about twelve seconds is the limit for most people!—which is a bit daunting. But time and again the man of God, the man who begins to be a saint, deliberately turns his thoughts to his Maker, until at last there are the 'brain paths' that lead him there all the time.

Let us determine to spend more and more time thinking about God—in prayer and meditation, until we too come to live with Him all the time. Mostly, our thoughts about God will be beneath the conscious surface; we *must* give full attention to our cooking or our account-books; we are not paid to sit and think about God and nothing else! But the thoughts will be there; 'hidden yet bright', and they will wonderfully influence all the other things we have to do and think about.

'And now, my friends,' says Paul (Phil. 4: 8), 'all that is true, all that . . . is just and pure . . . excellent and admirable—fill all your thoughts with these things.' Plato had said much the same many years before, except that it had not been revealed to Plato just how beautiful things really were. He had said, too, that we become beautiful by looking upon the beautiful, and in the broad sense that is true; the more we think the thoughts of beauty and peace, we pasture our souls in good fields; and the fruit for us is peace and strength.

What *do* you think about when you are alone, when there is nothing that you *must* think of? This is a deep question, a very important and revealing question. If you have the courage to face the answer, you will know a lot about yourself. When you sit in trains, especially those long coaches of the London Underground, it is interesting to watch the faces of your travelling companions. So many people reveal themselves, their secret worries and troubles, when their faces are in repose. How seldom do you see a face that is happy and serene! But what a blessing you get when you do! Sometimes a nun, or a young girl, or a man ripe in years, white of hair, carrying with him a dignity and a poise which speak of peace.

Learn to pray and to meditate. Start with a few Bible verses. If you don't know your way about your Bible, there are ways of getting help.[2] It was Canon Alan Richardson who said in one of his fine books that no one should pray until he had first read his Bible. How sensible! If we

[2] International Bible Reading Association; Bible Reading Fellowship; Scripture Union.

read the Word first, we turn to prayer with great things upon our minds. To read that 'God so loved the world . . .' is to be able to turn to the praise of so wonderful a God; and if you are interested in the world around us, or hear friends or members of your family talking about the wonders that science reveals, you will find greater wonder in science's wonderful 'First Cause' if you believe, as you may, that this same 'First Cause' is your loving Father in Heaven.

The voice that speaks in thunder
Says 'Sinner, I am Thine!'

There is an old story about a man whose friends left him sitting alone in a field while they went about their business. They were much delayed, and returned at last, loud in their apologies for leaving him so long. But he smiled and said, 'A couple of hours is no hardship when you've got God to think about.' He had *arrived*, and his thoughts could fly to the Father's heart like the homing pigeon; and it must be very wonderful to live like that.

4. *Step Out Into Life!*

It is many years now since J. B. Priestley made a sensation with a book called *The Good Companions*. It became at one stride a best-seller, and no wonder. To begin with, the book had a happy ending, and that has become a rare thing in books today (apart from popular love stories and detective novels). We may wonder what is happening to the stories people write. Much that is being produced is frankly indecent, and the writers seem to rejoice in putting down in close detail every unsatisfactory and unpleasant aspect of life. If you object, you are a 'prude' or old-fashioned; life is like this, say these writers, and that is how they are going to write.

It is not true that life is like that—for almost everyone there are more happy things in life than sad things; more things to be thankful about than to mourn or resent; more things to make us proud to be men and women than to be ashamed of. There are still some writers with the knack of setting down these happy or gracious moments; some writers of the other kind would call this sort of writing 'escapist': but it is a moot question if they themselves have not escaped *out* of life—perhaps because they have not the moral strength and fibre to face life's challenges and opportunities. Anyone who does not know the hopefulness that comes from belief in God may well find it easier just to lament or sneer than to 'have a bash' themselves!

The Good Companions covers a wide canvas; it has dozens and dozens of characters, and all are drawn with the warm human interest that makes J. B. Priestley so fine an artist. His books must have done much to declare life's true values and to encourage human helpfulness and comradeship, even though (one sadly knows) he does not seem led to be a Christian. But there are some wonderful people who will be most surprised 'at that day' to hear from God that they have been His servants!

The book has three principal characters. Miss Trant is the quiet and rather retiring daughter of old Colonel Trant, who has just died. She is thirty-five when the book opens, and is in the middle of all the upset involved in the sale of their West Country manor house. She decides to give herself a holiday, and drives off in a small car which she buys on an impulse (no driving tests when this book was written!). She has no idea what she will do or where she will go (except that a visit to Ely Cathedral seems foreshadowed, and her friend, the very human vicar, works out routes for her)—so that when she starts off, and the people who have bought her house want to know where they may find her if necessary, she shouts rapturously, 'No address!' and goes off rejoicing in this surprising and wonderful freedom. This is something that she has always wanted to do; and sweeping aside all fears and doubts, she is going to do it. (When Priestley wrote his book, a woman of thirty-five had 'settled down', with a place in the 'middle-aged' group—a position and a label that women of her age would cheerfully spurn today.)

Then there was Jess Oakroyd, from Bruddersford—a smoky Yorkshire town, the identity of which needs little probing. His full name was 'Jesiah', given to him during one of his father's sober periods, when he was apt to attend one of the big chapels of the town. Jess is married to a sharp-tongued and houseproud wife, and is more at home in his friend's shed than in the 'floor-polish' atmosphere of his own (or rather his wife's) house, and finds his chief happiness watching t'United. But even t'United often fails to satisfy; and Jess has dreams. He wants to see places—Bedfordshire, for instance. (Later he does see that pleasant county, and reflects that it looks much like any other place, which is true enough.) But one day, 'fed up' with the mills, he clambers on a lorry that is running down the Great North Road, and finds himself stranded in Nottinghamshire.

Miss Trant and Jess Oakroyd both have a dream of something better and more exciting that they have yet seen. They are not sure what they are looking for, but they feel, looking around them at their *very* ordinary days, that there should be something better than *this*. Life was surely intended to be inspiring and wonderful. Jess Oakroyd, as a blunt Yorkshireman, would hardly be able to put words like that together! But they say openly what he is dimly feeling inside him.

Yet a third character makes rendezvous with them. Lively young Inigo Jollifant, educated at Cambridge, is now a master in a third-grade Lincolnshire boarding school (the uncle of one of the boys dismissed the place with the words, 'It don't smell right'). His outlook on life seems frivolous and trifling to the Head, and more so to the Head's wife, and Inigo sets off from the wide Lincolnshire fields to seek his fortune elsewhere. Somehow these three all come into contact, and they also come into contact with a stranded concert-party—the 'Dinky-Doos', whose rascally manager has gone off with all the money (little enough) which the show has made. And over the hundreds of pages of the book we are shown how the concert party, renamed 'The Good Companions', taken over by Miss Trant, helped by Inigo's cheerful music and by the practical handyman ways of Jess Oakroyd, struggles through to success and to happiness, especially for Miss Trant, who meets a doctor who, years before, had made approaches and then drawn back. This time there is no drawing back and no mistakes.

If any of you have never read *The Good Companions*,

you have a genuine treat in store. The book, of course, is not religious in any sense. But there are many lessons about life and living; and there is a great message in this book. The main message can be expressed in the title of this chapter—'*Step Out Into Life*'. Life is waiting for you to greet it, and waits to greet you, and answer your dreams.

Very few people could do as Mr Priestley's three characters did, and drop all their present responsibilities and go off, and it would be wrong to urge you to try. In any case, there are adventures in quiet places, as we shall see in a moment. But there are many people who do stay dimly on in some place, not specially attractive, simply because they are there and lack a certain courage and faith. Visions come to us all until we crush them down, or until we forget that life does answer those who dare! Long ago, Abraham gazed night after night upon the wheeling stars in the great skies over the desert plains, until there came a feeling that something . . . Someone . . . was speaking to him; until at last 'Abraham went forth, not knowing whither he went' (Hebrews 11: 8), with very much about him changed, as well as his name.

Joan of Arc had her voices; and William Carey of Paulerspury, and Gladys Aylward of North London, too. Indeed, Christians believe that the same calls come to everyone, for we are all God's children, and equal in His love and in opportunity. They come to you and me from 'the Great Spirit' in so many ways—touches of beauty and the lives of others; happy things that were unforeseen . . . And the Voice behind them says, 'Be Alive!' Life is not just eating and drinking and working! There are marvellous things to do and be—if you will follow the gleam! The history books tell the stories of many who heard such a call and followed it. 'They desire a country.'

Most people, we saw just now, could not just drop everything and go off. If they did, others would suffer and be at loss. But the wonderful fact for the Christian is that there are many, many adventures of the spirit which we can taste while we remain in quiet places; and this can happen through the faithful discharge of things that we must do—often boring without this 'tincture', as George Herbert puts it, but shot through with eternal lovely meaning if we find the clue. If we pray that 'we may so pass through the things temporal that we finally lose not the things eternal'[3] we may also see that for us all these 'things temporal' are the way—the only way—to those eternal things. We shall be amazed, 'when the books are opened', to realize that some of life's greatest triumphs, as God measures triumphs, have been worked out in quiet places, and not in the broad highways and market-places of life. The man who conquers some sad inheritance in himself; the woman who spends her life for others, may stand higher than some of history's famous names. The thing that matters is God's call to you—and your answer.

Step out into life. Do what you are beginning to believe God wants you to do, even if nobody in your road has ever done it; even if all your friends feel that it is unsafe and rather strange. Pull yourself out of the rut. The new thing can always happen in a world like ours. A book by the great writer Tillich bears the title *The Courage to Be*; and there is a lesson in that title. It is wonderful how life answers the ventures and the dreams of those who *do* possess the courage to *be*. And the centre of the Gospel is *power*. Life answers to our strivings because life in its every part was made by Him.

[3] Collect of the Fourth Sunday after Trinity.

5. *Do You Read Advertisements?*

ADVERTISEMENTS surround us everywhere today: in the streets, on the Tube, in our newspapers, magazines, and TV. Indeed, Independent TV (just what is it 'independent' *of*?) could not continue without advertisements, any more than the newspapers could. It is surprising to realize that all this has grown up very largely in our lifetime. The art of advertising has grown amazingly since the makers of Pears' Soap surprised the world by taking a full page of *The Times* to say how good their soap was. They believed in advertising, and their slogan, 'Good morning. Have you used Pears' Soap?', amused some people very much, but annoyed others, who said it was a misuse of language. People argue about advertisements today in the same way—but that argument was very good for Pears' Soap, because everyone talked about it, one way or another!

Christians can learn much from advertising. There is actually a text that comes near to saying that God advertises! For in Romans 3: 25 the Greek words for 'whom God set forth' can very well mean 'whom God advertised'! Every Christian should be an advertiser! It is not only our ministers and preachers; much of the most effective work is done by ordinary people who are not preachers. Their friends listen to what they say because it's a friendly word and not formal—and especially because their friends live it as well as talk about it. 'O let me commend my Saviour to you!'—that famous hymn is for everyone, not just for preachers.

Let us see what the advertiser is trying to do, and see what this can teach us. Now, his real aim, the thing he spends his time and money on, is to persuade some one person to *do* something. Lots of 'ones', of course; but each one of them personally, himself. It takes months to get some advertisements prepared and printed, but at last there it is; an attractive picture, with some pointed wording, persuasive or funny: but will it do what they have been hoping? You will see a girl idly leafing over the pages of the 'glossy magazines' as you go on a train journey; but nearly always she just flicks the page over after the briefest moment in a way that would break the hearts of the talented men and women who have spent hours, days, designing it. It would surprise that girl—and you, perhaps—to know of the care and trouble involved in what they call 'lay-out', and in making up the 'blurbs' (the rather ugly word they use for the words of an advertisement), not to mention the search for just the right picture to set it off. the Pictures may take someone days to find, going to newspaper offices or agents or picture galleries . . . and the girl with the magazine looks at it all for perhaps three seconds, and turns the page over!

The advertiser has tried to make the advertisement really personal to the girl who turns over the pages. If he can use some words or some picture that will really get home to her, perhaps she *won't* turn that page over quite so quickly, and his word may really sink in! The advertisement is *public*; everyone can see it; and yet it succeeds only when some*one* acts upon its suggestions. If somebody who reads the advertisement actually goes to a shop and buys this article, the advertiser has got what he wanted; the thing he spent his money and his time for!

Surely the Christian can learn from this. We are not really saved in crowds, though there may be a crowd around us at the time when we really learn something about God for the first time. When anyone is converted it is all very personal:

Far was the call, and farther as I followed
Grew there a silence round the Lord and me.[4]

Isaiah knew it, one Saturday morning in Jerusalem, in a Temple that was probably crowded with people. Nobody else that we know of 'saw the Lord, high and lifted up' (Is. 6: 1) or heard Him say, 'Whom shall I send, and who will go for us?' (Is. 6 : 8). When this young man cried out from the depths of his being, 'Here am I, send *me*!', it was something absolutely between God and Isaiah. Have *you* come out of the crowd yet? The advertiser succeeds when some*one* takes his message and suggestion. Jesus is satisfied (Is. 53: 11) when, because of all He did and is doing still, some one man or woman says, 'Lord, I come!'

The advertiser wants you to do something *now*! Some advertisements have a little picture of a pair of scissors printed against the coupon which they want you to send in. The advertiser knows how it can be; you look at his advertisement, you are impressed, but . . . something happens—the postman, children home from school, a saucepan boiling over, and you forget about the advertisement for ever! Felix said to Paul, 'When I have a convenient season I will call for thee' (Acts 24: 25); but there is no evidence that the convenient season ever came. The Christian knows this danger. Time flies—how well we know that! 'The harvest is past, the summer is ended, and we are not saved!' (Jer. 8: 20). Charles Wesley knew this danger, and his songs often echo St Paul—'Behold, *now* is the accepted time; *now* is the day of salvation!' (2 Cor. 6: 2). Time and again in the early Methodist hymns and the early Methodist preaching we have the word 'Why not *now*?'

If anything impresses you, and you feel that you ought

[4] *St Paul*, F. W. H. Myers.

C

to do something about it—*do it now*! The best of impressions and intentions can fade.

Again, the successful advertiser believes in his goods—and tries to make you feel he does. You may have been in a shop when a traveller is there; you may have said, 'Oh, I'm not in a hurry', and waited while he finished his call. The man looks important, even benevolent; you feel that he wants to do good to everyone, and especially to this shopkeeper. He takes things out of his bag with obvious pride; you see that they are soap tablets, and he talks about this soap with obvious pride. You gather that there never has been soap like this before. You almost begin to pity yourself and all your friends; all these years you have been putting up with some inferior rubbish not worthy of the name of soap! Actually, you notice that the shopkeeper doesn't seem very much impressed by it all, and often the man packs his bag and goes out without a sale.

You smile; but think. The traveller sold nothing, yet there was always a chance that he might. But supposing he had come into that shop fearful, with a hang-dog air, and with a bag that he hardly dared to open. Supposing he had just said, 'Well: I've got some soap here; I don't know why you should buy it; it's no better than a dozen other soaps on the market; I can't guarantee that it will wash cleaner . . .' You saw the man talking proudly about his soap; he always had a chance; had he come in looking sheepish and ashamed, he would have wasted his time from the start. There are too many Christians today who are ready to talk about 'What's wrong with the Church'.

The great Christian evangelists have known that 'there is none other name under heaven . . . whereby we must be saved' (Acts 4: 12). Peter had already declared on the Day of Pentecost, 'There was nothing by which death could hold such a man' (Acts 2: 24, J. B. Phillips). That's the spirit! And on that wonderful day Peter's message was honoured when five thousand men joined the Christians. 'I am not ashamed of the Gospel of Christ,' said Paul (Romans 1: 16). Some scholars have wondered if this is a hint that some early Christians *were* ashamed of Him, and slow to tell others about Him. (Remember that He *had* died a criminal's death, and that the message said that nobody could satisfy God by themselves. Not many people would want to hear talk like that until they saw what was behind it.)

You can be proud of the Gospel; you can be proud of what God has done through His Church in two thousand years; proud of what He is doing today. Christians should have done more through the ages; but they *have* done more than others.

But now, something even more important. The firm that advertises may have a wonderful advertising man, and he may put together the most arresting advertisements. But . . . *the goods must live up to the advertisement*! If your new TV or radio set, made by that famous manufacturer, spluttered and flickered the whole time; if So-and-So's chocolate tasted gritty or worse; if the biscuits that look so appetizing in the coloured advertisement turned out to be tough and indigestible. . . !

The parable is very clear again here! Supposing that, one Sunday night, that thing happens for which all preachers pray and prepare—and which all congregations ought eagerly to expect—some bewildered stranger comes hesitatingly into the church and sits down on the first seat he can find. He is at the end of his tether, and he just wonders if there is anything in all this. And the service goes on, and the man in the pulpit begins to talk—and, by God's help, he talks so simply and attractively that the stranger begins to wonder, even to hope, that there is something *in* this . . . do you know what he is likely to do?

As the preacher speaks of the love and peace and joy of the Christian life, the stranger begins to look around him. These people—he supposes that they all believe what the preacher is saying; do they *look* like it? Ah! Time and again they do; there is an atmosphere of loving adoration and of joy in the Holy Ghost. And this is what *must* happen—and not only in church, but everywhere—and it does happen, even if it does not happen enough. In every generation there have been people who have gloriously shown that they are His, changed by Him. What was the use of the squire, the parson, or the magistrate telling an eighteenth-century village that the Methodists were rogues and hypocrites, when the people of the village saw them every day, and knew their kindness and goodness? When they saw the village drunkard and loafer turned from foul songs to cheerful hymns, and from evil living to clean living? The goods must back the sample.

Advertising has changed a lot in the last thirty years, but one kind works today as well as ever it did. Older people may remember the 'unsolicited testimonial'—generally for some kind of ointment—things like Zambuk! ('rub it in!'). It nearly always began, 'I feel that I must write and tell you. . . .' This is certainly an important line for the Church. When the ordinary man or woman sees a man in a clerical collar, they do one of two things—either get out of his way or, if escape is impossible, they behave rather unnaturally. They can't be themselves! But you—what an opportunity you have! They think that the priest or minister is bound to speak like that; anyway, it's his job! He's paid to! *You aren't*! Actually, if you talk about Jesus, you may be made to look silly; but it can make a very real impression.

There *is* room to *speak* about Jesus. Some Christians say, 'Oh, I can't speak about my faith: I try to live it.' Very good, too. Indispensable, in fact. But . . . some of these people do talk about everything else! A new soap, a good film, and they've plenty to say. Why not a word for Him, sometimes? It needn't be forced—and it won't have to be. Many a time a neighbour may say, 'Don't you get fed up with things!' and then you *can*, just quietly, pass on a word about what life has been for you since you knew Jesus.

Yes: the Christian is like the advertiser; he *is* an advertiser. Both have something to talk about; the advertiser for the sake of business, the Christian for love's sake. What a pity if people did more for money than for love! But there is one striking, even terrible difference. Nobody can *make* a man advertise. The newspapers and magazines and TV would like to, but they can't. *But the Christian is always advertising*—one way or the other. He can't help it. People watch—they watch you: you might be almost terrified to realize how they watch.

> *You are writing a gospel, a chapter a day,*
> *With the things that you do, and the words that you say;*
> *Men study the pages, the false and the true;*
> *Say—what is the Gospel according to . . . you?*

That sort of Gospel gets a bigger congregation than all the sermons.

The Christian cannot live in the shadow; he lives in a fierce blaze of light (Matt. 5: 13–16). Isn't this why we must pray constantly to Him, that we may truly 'add lustre to the doctrine' (Titus, 2: 10, NEB)? And what a joy it becomes!

6. *The Easiest Thing To Do*

THE duties of a chairman of a meeting have been defined as 'Speak up and shut up!', and perhaps a writer is most appreciated when he says plainly what he means, and says it quickly, too. 'I will not deceive you, my lord,' says Mrs Bardell, in *Pickwick Papers*; to which the judge replies, 'You had better not, madam!' I will not deceive you, either. The easiest thing to do in the world is . . . *nothing*.

Felix knew this when, having called St Paul and talked with him, he said, 'That will do for the present; when I find it convenient, I will send for you again!' (Acts 24: 25, NEB). St Paul had come a bit close as he talked to the Governor and seemed keen to make him a Christian too. Felix never did find it convenient to be converted to Jesus; to have the heart-to-heart talk with St Paul that might have made all the difference. The easiest thing to do is . . . nothing.

Actually, this is all about dentists; but nobody would have liked to start abruptly with *that*! For most people, this is a subject best left in the background until the evil day really comes. There are, of course, some who still follow the good old rule of going to see their dentist every six months, whether they actually need to or not. These are very wise people. It was a man like that who used to say, 'Some people are afraid to go to the dentist; I'm afraid *not* to go!' Very sensible, too, but how few people are so sensible.

Most of us are cowards about our teeth. We do not disagree with the man who described them as nature's chief mistake; and so many people put off the evil day. One look in the glass, one enquiring poke of the tongue, would make it clear enough that we need to see the dentist; so . . . we don't look, and we don't poke. And, of course, there are always such extremely good reasons for not going *today*! Tomorrow, perhaps . . . Stephen Leacock tells us about a visit to his dentist—he did at least get there. When the man looked like 'doing it now', Leacock made all sorts of excuses. There was something special to be done that very day, *and* tomorrow, *and* the day after that, *and* . . . until the dentist said firmly, 'You come tomorrow morning at ten o'clock!' The dentist had met people like Stephen Leacock before.

To tell the truth, we are much the same with many things. Anything awkward, unpleasant, difficult—we'd rather not think about it now! If, while we are talking about ordinary things, one of the big things of life or death suddenly breaks through, most people try hurriedly to avoid such talk with some easy word or joke. 'When I find it convenient . . . I will talk about that!'—which means 'Not now!'

St Augustine, the most brilliant man of his time, and (in his early days) one of the worst, was often tired of the life he was living, and often disgusted with himself. He had left his saintly mother's words and warnings far behind; but, doing what he liked, he did not often like what he did. 'The pleasures of sin' were proving far from pleasing. (In passing, if the people who have turned their backs on Christianity looked happier about it, we might wonder if they had done the right thing—but, as it is . . . !) One day, Augustine tells us, he got on his knees and prayed. It must have been years since he had prayed, if ever; and he started, 'O God of my mother . . .' as though God was better acquainted with his mother Monica than with him, and as though God would be more likely to do Monica a good turn! 'O God of my mother . . . make me pure . . . but not yet!' Well: nothing much happened

to Augustine. It took a different sort of experience to set
him on the road to real life.

The easiest thing in the world to do is . . . nothing.

But, sooner or later, people begin to see that something
is troubling us, and we have to confess that it is *teeth*.
We may have been lying awake with the pain, and we are
generally out of sorts. At last the truth is out; we have a
tooth that needs attention. And the moment you talk
about it, your friend knows just what to do. *He* knows a
dentist; a marvellous man. He could take all your teeth
out, let alone that one, without you feeling a thing. *He*
went to him some time ago now, and it was wonderful.
You go to see *him*. . . .

It is the same with colds. A minister with a cold, or
other people who call at a lot of houses, hear about 'a
wonderful cure' at nearly every house—a different one!—
and probably stay alive because they ignore the lot. But
while all this is being said, and with such enthusiasm,
the minister sometimes wishes that he might hear that man
or woman talking with the same enthusiasm and zeal about
Jesus and His gospel. We get lots of chances to talk about
Jesus if we really want them. We should never—or hardly
ever—seek to force this, but many a conversation brings
the opportunity. Here is a test; bear this word in mind
for a week, and you will notice a dozen opportunities to
speak about God to someone who would be all the better
for it! But we are shy about things like this; and (you
will see during this next week) we just crush it down
inside us. Our friend, or neighbour, would smile, or turn
the conversation, or she would think that we are a bit
strange . . . so nothing happens. What a pity that we can
contain our enthusiasm for Him, when we are ready to
recommend so many other good things!

But at last we are in such a state, we have suffered so
much pain, that we do fix an appointment. Off we go,

near the time arranged. We had never noticed that the journey to the High Street was so short; we are there at the dentist's before we realize, and in we go. It isn't so bad, we find, even though we suspect that this could be the courage of despair! We *are* there, and we know him, and he knows us. We don't see any need to point out all the bad places that we know of; we almost hope that he won't notice some of them! But he is noticing everything that is imperfect and is planning what to do.

Some dentists say at a certain point, 'This is going to hurt!', but sooner or later anyway we get that stab of pain. It can't be helped, and somehow when we brace ourselves for it, we can stand it; the moment passes, and we are still in one piece! The point really is that we trust the dentist to see us through. Perhaps in life itself, the bitterest sorrows and disappointments would be tolerable— more tolerable—if we truly trusted God. 'Lord, couldn't you save me from this?' It is a human cry; yet we reverently remember the cry that came from the holiest human lips ever: 'Not as I will, but as Thou wilt' (Matt. 26: 39). It must be the same for us. Can't we trust God, if we have learned to trust the dentist?

Nowadays, a dentist will save a tooth at all costs, and most of us prefer it that way. But if a tooth is diseased, if it would endanger other teeth or even the patient's entire health, out it comes! The dentist will have no truck with such a fifth columnist! 'If thine eye offend thee, pluck it out!' 'Offend'—cause to stumble, it means.

There are so many nice things in life that we need to be careful about. They are not wrong in themselves— nothing that God has made could be. But good things can still be dangerous. Music is surely one of God's gifts, but if a young man goes to concerts night after night, when he ought to be studying for the examinations that will qualify him for his career, God's gift of music is getting in his way. If you are watching your weight carefully there are some foods that you will avoid. They are *very* nice (that is the trouble!), but they are not for you. If some of the pleasant things of life hinder us from our proper business we shall have to do without them. Jesus our Lord was always out for business; and He is out for business to this very day. If we are out for business, we shall make time (Paul talks of 'buying up the time') for things that we have dreamed of.

Just one other thing—very obvious, but surely worth stressing—*no one else can go to the dentist for you*! Oh, yes; that *is* obvious; but there is point in the thought. So much of life is 'put out' today; you may remember the famous advertisement, 'Let the laundry do it all!' You can get most things done for you—if you will pay. But hardly any of the deepest and most real things are like that. No one else can pass *your* examination. No one else can be converted for *you*. Sometimes, indeed, we may understand the truth that every one of us is really alone, with deeps that the most sympathetic friend cannot really feel. We must do the big things for ourselves. Just as each one of us finds himself sooner or later in the dentist's chair, and just as this is a job that you simply can't put off; so each of us will find himself one day in the presence of God— answerable for life. When Peter wanted to know if there was to be some special treatment for John, Jesus answered him, gently but plainly, 'What is that to thee? Follow *thou* Me!' And it is so for each one of us.

But what a marvel of His grace that each of us can also put his hearty trust in Christ his Saviour, and thus be ready 'at that day'.

> *Bold I approach the eternal throne*
> *And claim the crown through Christ, my own!*

7. *The Light Shines in the Darkness*

You may have been to see the Eddystone Lighthouse; and if you have, you will have admired it—and also those who built it, and those who serve it. Certainly, thousands upon thousands of sailors have been thankful for the light that streams so constantly to help them. This is a work that is not much in the public eye, but which must go on. Most of us, and our newspapers, think only of these devoted men when six-week storms have stopped their supplies!

As a building, the present Eddystone is much less impressive than an earlier lighthouse—the second one they built there. That lighthouse was a really handsome job, with a lot of beautiful and effective decorations, scrolls and ornaments of ironwork. Visitors came to admire it from all parts of the land, and everybody said, 'Now, *that*'s what a lighthouse should look like!'

But not *so* many visitors, as it turned out. Because, not very long after they had put it up, it fell down.

Well, the main point about a lighthouse is that it does stand there to show a light! And they went very thoroughly into the question why this one hadn't. They drew certain conclusions—and when they began again, everything was streamlined and sheer. Nothing for the winds and storms to take hold of. The present Eddystone lighthouse stands today because it follows the same rule. It is a simple, elemental building, with nothing unnecessary about it.

Simplicity is always best. When a man says with Paul, 'This one thing I do!', his life has a directness and a simplicity which give real strength to all he is and does.

Which end of a lighthouse matters most—the foundations or the light? You can see the point of the question.

If there is no light, the lighthouse might as well not be there. But if it won't stand up, there is little use in the 'top end' being in perfect working order!

Many years ago, some people came from Germany to get details of the great Philharmonic Hall in Liverpool. With true German thoroughness they noted every conceivable measurement and fact; and the building they erected in Germany was in every way a faithful copy of the Merseyside hall. But what a shock when the orchestra first rehearsed for a concert! The sounds were distorted and imperfect; as a concert hall it was hopeless. Back they went to Liverpool to check their measurements and their details. They went over everything again, but they were completely puzzled. Everything was quite correct. At last a wise man realized what had happened. They had faithfully copied the famous Liverpool hall; but the foundations were not the same, and so the materials did not respond in the same way. We might find all the technical details rather difficult, but we can understand this broad fact and reason.

Foundations matter. The hidden things matter. One day the word goes round a town, 'Have you heard . . . ?' A leading citizen of the place has fallen into disgrace and dishonour. Men have admired him, and not a few envied him. Yesterday many looked up to him; today 'none so poor to do him reverence'. But these things do not really happen in a day. You are surprised, and even angry, when they come to cut down a great tree in its glory. You have loved that tree, perhaps, for years. But they show you that there is decay and rottenness inside it, and these have eaten its strength away. For a long time —tree and man alike—something has been attacking the foundations, wasting the hidden reserves, and though the crash seems to come in a moment, it is the end of a long story.

Yet surely the light *is* more important; or why a

lighthouse at all? It is a constant reminder and warning of danger. When we stand on the high cliff we watch the light as it flashes, every so-many seconds; what devotion, and often sacrifice, men show in maintaining their light! It is the one thing they are there for. The light must always shine: once there has been a light in that dangerous place it is essential to keep it going. If sailors do *not* see a light where they have learned to look for a light, they may very well land in disaster; for if nothing warns them off, they will think that they are safe so far.

In all this there is much for the Christian to think about. His only task is to witness to his Lord. Sometimes, that can mean death itself. When that happens we call the man a 'martyr', which is the Greek word for 'witness'. More often, to witness for Him means living steadily and patiently. You don't have to force yourself on others, or obtrude; the lighthouse gleam doesn't do that; it is just *there*. Whatever else the Christian does in life—run a great business, write fine poetry, score goals, or sweep roads, he knows that he is here to *witness*. 'O let me commend my Saviour to you!', sings Charles Wesley. There are millions of quiet, glad Christians in the world who try to live like that. Samuel Pepys made a careful check of his money and his goods at the end of each year, writing it all carefully in his account book, and devoutly thanked God if he had more than he had last time! But the only book that the Christian is really interested in is called 'The Lamb's Book of Life'. He measures his success in life by his success in bringing others to God, though often he does not know what his success has been.

It is a sad thing when the man with the name of Christian lives an unreal, selfish life! If the lighthouse fails to give its warning or its guiding sign, hundreds may be in peril. The man who is a Christian in name only, who is unworthy of his Lord, can bring ruin! People are so ready to justify themselves by others' failures. 'I don't *pretend* anything,' they say virtuously—as if it had ever been a virtue to live without aiming at something!—cowardice, selfishness, more like! 'But' he goes on, 'all these people who look good have got another side if you look for it!' Many of these accusations spring from jealousy and are not true; but may God preserve us from failing Him in that way, and giving any man an excuse for an evil life. If our true reward when we reach Heaven is to see His look, and hear His word, 'Well done, good and faithful servant!' what would we feel if His look said, 'You made one of my little ones to fall!'? Here, surely, would be shame and sorrow never-ending; the very stuff of hell itself.

The Bible tells us that Jesus could be angry; indeed, His anger was the only real anger that earth has ever known, in all its blinding purity. In the anger of the best of men there is some trace of self and of prejudice. The anger of God is one of the foundations of the universe. Otherwise, life would not be so real and strong. Our Lord's anger flashes when anyone makes the 'little ones' to stumble. 'Little ones' in that context does not mean only those who are young in years; it means any who may be looking wistfully towards the possibility of a better life. If, at such a time, someone hinders or discourages them, our Lord would be truly and deeply angry. Surely, we should be grieved and ashamed to be a stumbling-block. The Greek word for 'stumbling-block' is *scandal*.

You will remember that the first Eddystone Lighthouse fell down. Small blame to the builders, you may think, when you remember the force of the winds and the unceasing challenge of the sea. The sea makes a bold frontal attack; and you could almost imagine, when you see it, that the defiance of the lighthouse provokes the sea to a greater fury. Perhaps the other challenge of the sea is even more dangerous. The second lighthouse gave no chances to the wind and the storm, but it had to be replaced because the sea had undermined the rocks on which it stood. Just how does a lighthouse stand up, anyway?

Well: the builder of the second lighthouse, and the great Smeaton who built the third, made a special study of this problem. It could be said that the lighthouse stands because every stone is welded into a unity with every other stone. At no point does a single stone meet the sea's challenge and attack. The stones are dovetailed into one another, and then stout wooden wedges are driven in between. After this, strong 'nails', also of wood, are inserted between and through the stones. So, when the waves lash and the storm is high, it is a *unity* which shudders together and which yet withstands. Any one stone can, of course, be the first to meet the attack, but the sea's force crashes and shivers away over and through the whole mass of the foundations and the building. Finally, the stout firm rock on which the lighthouse stands receives the rude force and shock.

What a fine image of the true Christian community, and of the strength which each single Christian can find in the family! 'Bear ye one another's burdens,' says Paul (Gal. 6: 2). In a true church, a true society, the members do bear one another up. They remember one another in prayer; there is encouragement and understanding. There are the little practical things with which we can help, so that it is not wrong to think of a cup of tea, and the friendship that goes with it, as sacramental. Above all, each single one, and the whole friendly society, is set deep in the Rock—Christ the Rock. The rocks into which the lighthouse is deeply set can be undermined and can shift; but we are 'grounded on the rock which naught can move'.

No lighthouse by itself could oppose the full fury of the gale. But it does not need to. It is built into the rock. So we are upheld by our Saviour. He knows the full weight of the blast, and He knows the incessant challenge of all that would oppose and undermine—'for He hath felt the same'.

8. *Burning Your Boats*

EZRA was a very worried man. The Bible calls him (Ezra 7: 6) 'a ready scribe in the law of Moses'—the best name for him today would be 'a leading civil servant'. He lived in very important days, and was able to go straight to the great King of Persia in order to ask a very big favour.

That favour was 'Please, may the Jews go back home?' They had been taken to Persia after a war that they lost, and they always longed to get back to Jerusalem. 'If I forget thee, O Jerusalem, may my right hand forget its cunning!' (Ps. 137: 5).

'You *can* go back, Ezra, with your people,' said the great King, very graciously. 'But it's a very dangerous journey—are you going to be all right?'

'Your Majesty,' said Ezra, 'our God—Jehovah is His Name—is the greatest of all gods, and He will see us safely through. That's really why we want to get back—Jerusalem is the proper place to worship Him.' And so it was all arranged.

But many other things needed to be arranged, too. It was a very wonderful thing that they could go back where they longed to be. But what a lot of work for Ezra! There were all the Jews who wanted to return, with their families, including lots of children, to be set in marching order. The Bible does not tell us, but it is very likely that they would take a lot of cattle with them. Lots of children, and lots of cattle; anyone who has had anything to do with a Sunday School treat knows just how many things can happen when you are trying to get organized.

Imagine this great company of people, and herds of cattle, and a convoy carrying the precious gold and silver things which the Persian King and his people had given them: and just then, one of his friends came up to Ezra.

'Ezra,' he said, 'it's going to be a difficult journey. Hundreds of miles across these barren desert lands. There are thieves and violent men out there. Oughtn't we to ask the King for some soldiers to go with us?'

It must have sounded very sensible, too! But you may see just what Ezra's difficulty was. He had told the King of Persia that the Jews served the great God, and that He would keep them safe whatever happened. It would have looked rather strange after that if he had gone back and asked for some soldiers! 'I was ashamed to ask,' he says (Ezra 8: 22). And he didn't. After a time of prayer they started off.

How slow their journey must have been. The proverb says that an army marches at the speed of its slowest member; and this 'army' had some very slow members. Mothers, especially mothers with little children, and women who are expecting to be mothers, can't move very quickly, and the cattle would be slow. The journey would be about nine hundred miles, and it took them a hundred and eight days! And all that time, moving slowly over the desert, they were open to attack from robbers and marauders. Time and again they must have said, 'Wish we'd got some soldiers with us!', and however bravely Ezra bore himself, he must have had a sinking feeling inside when, perhaps, his keen ears could discern the movements of raiders somewhere in the darkness around them. But they were not attacked; they got through safely, and they arrived with rejoicing in Jerusalem.

Our title is 'Burning your Boats', and you can see the picture behind the words. Men have sailed over wide and dangerous seas, and at last they have reached land. They have no idea what lies in those unknown fields and forests; they do not know what enemies they are going to find. There might be some sense in bringing their boats up on to the shore, so that, if things are too bad in the new country, they can race back to the shore and get away. But once they have burned their boats, they must take what comes, for better or for worse.

Ezra trusted his God, and (like everyone who really trusts God) he was not let down.

Along the Euston Road in London, opposite the great railway station, there is a fine building called the Friends' House. It is the headquarters of the Quakers, who really call themselves 'Friends', only everyone else calls them Quakers, just as the Methodists know that their name was a nickname and a sneer to start with. But both the Quakers and the Methodists have lived that down, and made their name something to be proud of. In the Friend's House there is a special picture. It shows a Quaker meeting-house in America during the eighteenth century. A company of Red Indians is bursting into the little meeting-house, in full war-paint and waving their tomahawks. The Quakers in the picture are sitting perfectly still, perfectly quiet.

A tablet on the picture-frame tells the story of how the Red Indians just stole away, leaving the Quakers unharmed, because, as they said afterwards, they felt that 'The Great Spirit was there.' We can imagine that the silence of the Quakers was a special kind of silence. If it had been that terrified sort of silence of people who were just frozen with fear, it would almost certainly have been the end of the Quakers! For the Red Indians would have sensed this, just as a dog seems to know when people are afraid, and bothers them, whereas if you treat him calmly he will just trot off. But those Quakers knew that God was there, and were sure that He would protect them. Actually, in such a case, the real Christian would probably feel that even if he and his friends were going to be killed, it would still be best to remain quiet in God's presence. As it was, the

Red Indians were impressed by the strong calm peace of it all.

These Quaker men and women certainly knew the true way of peace. The sight and sound of the Indians must have been as alarming to them as to anyone else, but, like Ezra, they trusted God. But what a practical way to live! They believed the Bible promises. Most people would say, 'Impossible!', but it really worked, not once, but many times. Say, if you like, that it was just coincidence—they believed that it was all the work of a God who *cared*.

And, remember, this was 'trusting God' in very practical things. God's care is ours, not only in what we call 'religious' things, but in everything we do each day—the 'practical' things as well. Certainly Ezra, leading an army of ordinary people slowly over the desert, or the Quakers sitting there with Red Indians around them, were living real life. But they trusted God, and He brought them through.

Do *we* turn to God in our problems? That does not mean doing nothing; it means just the opposite. It means being quiet and faithful, and just getting on with our duty. Anxiety is like rust; it eats away our energy and strength. We sometimes sing

> *I am trusting, fully trusting*
> *Sweetly trusting in Thy Word.*

If we give our all to God, He gives His all to us. In *The Imitation of Christ*, by Thomas à Kempis, you will read the words 'God gives His blessing when He finds an empty vessel'; and those words are worth pondering. You have heard people talk about 'swimming with one foot on the bottom'. Well: that isn't swimming, but, furthermore, it isn't restful, either. Just imagine the picture, of a man half-swimming in that way, and compare it with the peace and restfulness of the man who floats on the surface of the sea: fully supported and fully quiet.

Do we, then, turn to God in our problems? Do we, while doing all that we can and ought, wait to see what God will do for us and with us? If so, our religion is coming real.

It is a wonderful experience when things come real. Ordinary things, to start with. You've often thought about having a holiday abroad, and you pore over the coloured books they send you, and you make your plans, and you get your passport and all the needed papers . . . until one day it's not a matter of looking at the pictures in a book; you are actually sitting there on the beach, or climbing that mountain, or enjoying that marvellous view—this is really *us* and we are really here! It's the same with a lot of other experiences, happy and otherwise, that will occur to you. We've often read about this, or seen other people in this—but now we are here ourselves.

It is even more wonderful when Bible promises really come true; when it isn't just something printed on a page, but something that I am really feeling. We find this sort of thing even in the Bible itself. 'When the Lord turned again the captivity of Zion,' says the writer of the 126th Psalm, 'we were like unto them that dream!' Like us, they had often heard about God, and the priests and the prophets had spoken to them about God, and it all sounded very nice and very inspiring. But this is real—we're going home, back to Jerusalem after being prisoners! They heard the people living around them—perhaps some of *them* also prisoners, but who had *not* heard the word of release, saying enviously, 'Their God (Jehovah, they called him) has done great things for *them*!' And they replied joyfully and triumphantly, 'The Lord *hath* done great things for us!' This is religion coming true in life, and it is a wonderful thing. It is what John Wesley knew,

and Mary Slessor, and Gladys Aylward, and thousands
upon thousands of others.

It's the only way to find real happiness, and to live the
life you've dreamed of. Go on with a good heart, doing
what you know you ought. Most of the time we don't need
a special message from God to tell us what to do; the Bible
gives us wonderful help in living, and the Church after
two thousand years has a lot of experience and has done
a lot more than some people think. We know, for instance,
that it is always better to be kind than cruel; to be
unselfish rather than selfish, and that the Ten Command-
ments still stand. If we find ourselves up against something
rather difficult and unusual we can ask God for special
help with *that*, and it will come—often through another
man or woman rather than through wonderful voices and
visions! Through something we see or hear. But it will
be God's voice. And all the time we are looking towards
God. 'Mine eyes are ever towards the Lord' (Ps. 25: 15),
more and more like Ezra. Our trust will be in God, and
we will not fear what man can do. Our strength comes
from the Lord (Ps. 121: 2), and every day shows us how
sufficient that is.

9. *Wait For It!*

MANY years ago now, people flocked to the Albert Hall in London to see *Elijah*, the famous oratorio by Mendelssohn. This is a wonderful piece of music, as you may know, and although 'the clever people' declare mockingly that it is very old-fashioned and not worth attention, the rest of us still go gladly whenever it is performed. Great songs like, 'If with all your hearts', 'Woe unto them that forsake Him', and 'O come, everyone that thirsteth' are part of most people's memories, and they give strength and comfort in difficult times.

But that word about *seeing Elijah* is a bit unusual. It is the right word, though; people listened, as usual, of course; but the great oratorio was being given in costume, and a very lively affair they made of it. It is not normal to see coloured balloons floating around the arena of the Royal Albert Hall, except perhaps at the start or finish of a Promenade Concert season, or on the great night once a year when the Methodist Association of Youth Clubs fills the Hall, and anything can happen! (MAYC *does* fill the Hall; so that it looks as if some young people do go to church, despite what the newspapers say!) Coloured balloons were very prominent that night, when they gave *Elijah* in costume. The producers of the concert wanted to show the effect of Queen Jezebel and her followers upon the more sober Jewish court and people, and the costumes were brilliant.

Gay clothes and striking costumes, then—but one of the greatest scenes was very drab indeed. In the whole expanse of that great oval arena, where you can often see a great crowd of excited youngsters enjoying a Promenade Concert, and at other times hundreds of chairs seating

55

row after row of people in a dignified assembly, there was just one figure—and that figure dressed in coarse sacking, lying in a huddled heap to one side. The floor of the arena was covered with some sort of material that gave a good impression of the sandy desert. It was such a change. Earlier on, the fierce excitement of the battle between God's one lone prophet, Elijah, and the priests of Baal; then Elijah's reaction of disheartenment, natural, perhaps, after these fierce scenes. He had sung, 'It is enough; O Lord, now take away my life, for I am not better than my fathers!' Then (you can read this wonderful story in 1 Kings, chapter 19) 'he lay down and slept under a juniper tree.' Suddenly, then, in this costume performance, three angels were there in serene blue dresses (their sudden appearance startled some people). They sang 'Lift thine eyes . . . thy help cometh from the Lord. . . ', and soon the tense audience was listening to perhaps the loveliest of all the songs (or 'arias') in *Elijah*: 'O rest in the Lord; wait patiently for Him'.

Those words come from the Psalms (37: 7), of course, not from the Elijah story in the book of Kings; but Mendelssohn's instinct was right—or perhaps we should say, the instinct of good Pastor Schubring, who provided Mendelssohn with the words.

'O rest in the Lord; wait patiently for Him.' These words must have appealed deeply to Mendelssohn for him to have clothed them with such beautiful music. And they are a wonderful answer to human sorrows and cries and protests. 'O rest in the Lord' is, we saw, a word from the Psalms; but left to themselves men are more likely to utter another word from the same book (Ps. 119: 126), 'It is time for the Lord to work!' In the days of King Stephen and of Queen Matilda, soon after the Norman Conquest, things were so terrible in this land for ordinary men and women that 'men said the Christ and His saints slept.'

Why doesn't God *do* something? So many times in human history that cry has gone up; and so many times it has seemed that surely God must do something *now*. . . . He does not—or so it seems. If we could see everything we should understand that He is working towards some wonderful thing that we shall see in His good time. But it *will* be in *His* good time—and He knows best.

'It is time for the Lord to work.' We can't help saying that, when we see evil men getting away with something wrong, and hear them mocking and sneering at the good. Psalm 73 gives a remarkable picture of such people; the words of our indignant psalmist etch them unforgettably in a picture that is completely up-to-date. 'They say, "*How* doth God know?" ' At such times the indignation of good men is surely not wrong, and they are sure that 'it is time for the Lord to work.' Well: for our comfort and encouragement, let us remember this. He wants to. He is often far more anxious than we are. The story of our Lord's crucifixion shows that; and we truly believe, with the hymnwriter, that the Cross just revealed in a moment of time what has always been going on in God.

> *But even could I see Him die,*
> *I could but see a little part*
> *Of that great love which like a fire,*
> *Is always burning in His heart.*

He *wants* to come to the relief of His children. But He knows the best time; and perhaps it is not yet. So we must 'rest in the Lord; wait patiently for Him'; and even though we find tears, we shall find this way best for us.

We can gladly believe that a loving God wants the best for us; if that good thing does not come just now, may we not trust Him, and believe that the time is not ripe? In so many human affairs we often have to *wait*; hurry is vain; could this teach us the lesson we need for the

greater things of life and eternity? The man who is making
his garden path knows that the cement must have time to
harden. Modern skill—or modern impatience—certainly
brings about some speedier results; paint dries more
quickly than it used. But we do still have to wait until
things are ready. The mother who has made a pie, and
is complimented when the family stand round the kitchen
sniffing like Bisto kids, and saying, 'When can we have
some, Mum?', will be quite firm that it must stay there a
long while yet; and woe betide anyone who dared to open
the oven door to see how things were going! Our impatience with the things of life is often rather like trying
to open the oven door, and is equally foolish. If we really
want to understand things, we should hold our peace and
our patience.

But is there sometimes another reason why God does
not work the marvels we are waiting for? 'It is time for
the Lord to work'—are there times when He would do so,
but we are not really listening, not really ready? 'The
Master calleth thee!' (John 11). Mary was ready—all
the readier because she had a habit of sitting quiet.
Perhaps if it had been Mary who first met Jesus, and she
had gone back with a message for Martha, she would have
been clattering about with things and might never have
heard the summons. (Most of us have a strong sympathy
with Martha in *that* story; but that is another matter!)
We are often like Martha. 'The world is too much with
us.' Or else we do not realize that He seeks to help us.
There is many a time when the baby cries, and splits the
welkin with his shrieks. All the time, if only he would
stop his bawling, probably with his eyes shut tight, he
would see waiting for him something that he wants, or
something better than he had thought of. So long as he
laments, he will be the loser—and so shall we! Have you
ever tried to rescue a kitten out of a tree? All you want to

do is to help the kitten, and to get it out of its awkward
situation; but you can't get the poor thing to believe it—
he will lash out in fear at the hand you extend to help.
(Perhaps our fear of death is this same sort of 'needless
fear', as Paulus Gerhardt calls it in his hymn? So many
people seem to meet their last moments in great peace.)

'Rest in the Lord; wait patiently for Him.' There is
much evidence that it is foolish to seek to force God's
hand by some sudden or impatient act of your own.
Things will certainly go wrong if you try that. We do
best to hold on in prayer, and to do the straightforward
and ordinary things that we know have got to be done,
like getting the children their breakfast or going to see
the old friend who does so depend on your visits, and
for the rest to 'wait patiently'. Light will come when God
sees best. These things are not easy, but they are right.
When we try to 'help things on' we often do the wrong
thing, and later on we wish we hadn't taken a hand.

Something very important must be added, though. We
must understand very fully that this is not a call to the
dull resignation that so easily becomes loth and mere
inaction. The psalmist is thinking of a frame of mind that
leads to inward response and to action when at last God
does give the signal. This is the ideal; not a moment too
soon, but not a moment's delay when the call does come.

A motorist doesn't like to see the traffic lights at the
red when he approaches them; he would like to sail
through eternally on the green. If the red light does show,
he will respect it if he is wise—but have you noticed how
he sits? He has stopped; he is patient (or resigned!) but
he is all eagerness to go forward the moment he may.
(The other motorists behind him will help him to notice
when the green light shows, if he falls to thinking of other
things!) And the moment he *can* go forward, he *does* go
forward. When runners compete in a great race, the starter

will say 'Get set!', and they crouch at the starting-line, in such a bodily position that when the starter's gun gives the signal they can catapult themselves forward without a second's delay along the track.

It is a fine life that moves with the same obedience when God calls. There is a lot about sport in the Bible, and the Psalmist talks in Psalm 19 (v. 5) of the joy 'of a strong man to run a race'. No hesitations, no delay; 'at the ready'. Just as the runner wastes neither energy nor time, but uses every atom of both, so the Christian who fully trusts his God is saved so much of anxiety and worry. When his God calls, he will be ready. Before his God calls, he will not be anxious.

'Trust—and obey.' God's wisdom knows the time; and you will be ready. You have longed to be on the move; but you have trusted His wisdom and waited. When at last the sign truly comes, you will know what to do. *You* will rejoice like a strong man to run a race. All your effort will be eager, economical, effective.

We want more people who will 'rest in the Lord', and who will put dull care behind. There would be fewer discontented, anxious, and troubled faces in the streets and on our buses and trains. It is those who do 'rest in the Lord' who have the energy and the grace to respond when God's word comes. 'Ye have dwelt long enough in this mountain' (Deut. 1: 6). Well, we had rather thought that ourselves! But it was for You to say so. They've not wasted that energy before. Now it will be all movement, all effort, all courage, all eagerness, all battle, all triumph.

Sometimes, after a lesson session of acting, an actor will make it known that he is 'resting'. Resting is good for actors; they can recover their poise and their balance. People who rest, relaxed, are all the readier for the call when it does come.

The most wonderful example of this for all time was

shown when a quiet, serene girl . . . waited. We know nothing of her earlier life, but we may believe that it was ordinary and uneventful; her days came and went, busy in the simple duties of the village and the home. But one day, God's angel came to her, and told her that for her there was the unbelievable thing, the greatest destiny that ever woman faced. She was to have a child, and that child would be God's Son: all of God that a human frame could contain. She said quietly, 'Behold the handmaid of the Lord' (Lk 1 : 38), and went forward to her destiny in full faith and trust.

We may learn from her. 'Wait patiently for Him.' Trust in God enough to be quiet, not to waste your power by frittering it away in anxious care. Then you will be ready when the great day comes, and God's call sounds in your ears like the music of great trumpets—or when perhaps there is just the still small voice, just as dramatic and powerful. 'Wait patiently': 'Rest in the Lord': then, like Elijah in the days that followed, you will be ready when the time comes.

10. *Comfort?*

YEARS ago they used to advertise a very special kind of armchair. The picture showed a pair of knees, part of a body sunk well and deeply into the chair, roomy and comfortable. Underneath were the words, 'Get out of that chair, Kenneth!' Kenneth was, it appeared, the son of the family, and the general idea was that father had a right to sit in it, too. If you read on, you were given to understand that you had to buy one of these chairs (or perhaps two, if you couldn't get Kenneth to shift) to get relief from every worry. Here was perfect comfort. Here was rest from trouble. Well; we do all need comfort and rest from trouble. People took notice of these advertisements, and the firm made a lot of money.

A little while later another advertisement appeared. Big armchairs are all right, said this second advertisement, but, it added in very large letters, 'You don't get comfort in a big armchair!' Well, of course, you do; comfort of a sort. But the second advertisement was about insurance; and it *is* true that when you are sitting comfortably in your big armchair, you are even more comfortable (in mind as well as body) if you know that you have done all you can to prepare for the worst that may happen.

So many unexpected things can happen, of course. It is amazing and rather terrible, how trouble can come our way from people we have never seen or heard about. Here, in the luxurious lounge of a five-star hotel, which you would hardly dare to go into, with everything extremely quiet and discreet, sit two prosperous looking men, well dressed, and with the quiet authority that you see about really big business men. They talk for a while; they don't raise their voices; everything is very friendly;

there is no excitement and no argument. Then the news is out: one firm has 'taken over' another firm. It's all very business-like, and the financial columns of the newspapers quite approve (those columns that most of us pass over every morning): the solicitors and the accountants are well satisfied. But this is going to prove very awkward for perhaps thousands of ordinary men and women. They may have to move to another town, and leave friends and familiar places; they may find themselves doing different jobs, which they don't like, and may have to work with or under people they just can't get on with. All this can come at one stroke; in a moment. All those lives suddenly affected and altered because two men do some planning.

Here is a retired couple. They have saved hard through their earlier lives. Their dream was a bungalow in some quiet corner of a town they love. They got closer and closer to their dream, and now here they are. A few other houses near them, some trees, a garden that they tend and keep in order. One day the news comes round; men have been drawing maps and counting the traffic, and the Corporation are going to drive a road right through this quiet sanctuary. They may be good enough citizens to know that all this is necessary for the good of their town and for their fellow-citizens; but they will surely feel a bit rueful about it.

'You don't get comfort in a big armchair.' You don't get guaranteed comfort even from insurance, if you get involved in the sort of situations we have just been considering. No insurance company would insure your nice bungalow against the risk of a new development that would spoil all its quiet. There are, of course, situations where insurance can help a lot . . . that is, if the insurance company itself keeps out of trouble! You might ask the general manager of the insurance company, 'Are you *sure* that your "comfort" is quite guaranteed? Will your company always be there, when I want some help? Insurance companies have gone bankrupt, you know!' And you ask him about wars, or riots, or the failure of his own investments. There could come a day when the biggest and most important insurance company ran into trouble. It's not *very* likely, because all the insurance companies help one another, so that no one need be very alarmed about all this. But if a man is looking for something absolutely sure, what does he really do? Certainly the insurance company seems able to offer better comfort than the comfort of the big armchair; but isn't there something missing still?

How do you ensure that nothing awkward or unpleasant will ever come your way? How can you make it certain that life will always be agreeable, calm, and happy?

The answer is very simple, and very brief. You can't.

And yet nearly everyone of us will know someone—perhaps just some*one*—who seems to live in an atmosphere of calm, that nothing seems to shake or disturb. When we are uncertain about the future, it unsettles us—and that is where most of us lose a lot of energy, and a lot of time. Really, although the old 'Wayside Pulpit' message is just about threadbare now: 'Don't worry—it may never happen!', it still has its point, and we all admit this as we look back. It didn't happen, but we did worry.

That's all very well!' you say, 'but we never knew it *wasn't* going to!' Now, that man or woman you thought of just now would smile, or shake their heads, if you suggested that no troubles ever came their way or ever threatened them—and you may happen to know that they have had their share. But these people certainly make us all feel better. We want more of them. A paper in Boston, America, said one morning, 'The city (meaning the business quarter) was looking very dull yesterday—and Phillips Brooks walked through!' He was the minister of a leading Boston church: but the mere sight of him did you good; you didn't have to wait to hear him preach! Charles Lamb loved to see the Quakers come 'in their shining bands' to the May Meetings in London—even if their plainness and downright speech rather disturbed him.

These people have something—but what? Something more than comfortable armchairs—though they do have these as well if they are wise! Something more than insurance—though most of us do what we can about *that*. But what is it that is special to them? Has something given them the assurance that nothing disagreeable, nothing awkward or tragic, shall ever happen to them? No. They have something better than that.

Into their lives has come the quiet feeling that whatever does come, they can meet it without fear—they can 'take it', as we say. They do, of course, wonder what is coming, like the rest of us, because they are human, and like us they try to read the signs of the times. But they have this deep feeling that nothing will happen that they won't somehow get through, though they couldn't tell you how, at this moment.

If a man is a millionaire he doesn't worry about paying his gas bill! He would know that he can, whatever it comes to. Actually that isn't a very good illustration, for some people who are very well off got that way through watching their expenses! But you will get the idea behind it. There are people who are certain about life. They are not specially brave; they don't like pain, or disappointment, or sorrow any more than anyone else. But there is something that keeps them calm and practical when things are difficult, or look like being difficult.

In Jeremiah's seventeenth chapter there is a sermon on the First Psalm. Jeremiah quotes David's words, and then enlarges upon them. 'Blessed is the man that trusteth in the Lord . . . for he shall be as a tree planted by the

E

waters, and that spreadeth out his roots by the river, and
shall not fear when heat cometh, but his leaf shall be
green; and shall not be careful in the year of drought,
neither shall cease from yielding fruit.' That is a beautiful
picture from nature. This tree doesn't have to fear, and
it will not be unfruitful; its roots are by the river.
Jeremiah's sermon shows us the secret.

The people we were talking about, whose calm and
strength we admire and envy, don't do it by themselves.
Nobody can. But they have joined themselves to God, and
God's power is with them. 'The Lord is the strength of
my life—of whom shall I be afraid?' (Psalm 27). As the
days go by, their experience strengthens their faith.

When David wanted to face Goliath, the giant, Saul
tried to dissuade him. 'Thou art but a youth, and he a
man of war.' David's answer was to the point. 'I was
watching my father's sheep a while ago now; and if a lion
or a bear came after the flock, and stole a lamb, I went
after him and got it back. I killed the lion and I killed
the bear. Now I am ready to face this giant of a man.'
What David is really saying is something that could help
us. He says, 'Well: I've scored a hundred per cent so far
in what I've had to face—and that's a good start for facing
something else!'

This is what John Newton means when he sings,

> *His love in time past forbids me to think*
> *He'll leave me at last in trouble to sink;*
> *While each Ebenezer I have in review*
> *Confirms His good pleasure to help me quite through.*

So we can be sure on three levels; and only one really
lasts. Some people make a science of comfort, and really,
for our few moments of leisure, why not? The comfortable
armchair, the draught-stopper, the cushions carefully and

cleverly placed; surely this will give us some ease—and it does. But it can still leave the mind in trouble. Some of this unrest will vanish if we are wisely insured. But there are things that could wreck insurance—wars or national or world disturbances. So, thirdly, I have *true* comfort when I can say, and only when I can say:

> *E'en let the unknown tomorrow*
> *Bring with it what it may:*
> *It can bring with it nothing*
> *But He will bear us through.*

'I know Him Whom I have believed,' says Paul (2 Tim. 1: 12), another man who knew trouble and difficulty and opposition (read 2 Corinthians 11: 23–29) '... and I am persuaded that He is able to guard that which I have committed unto Him against that day'.

Only at this point, then, does comfort become final and complete. It is the assurance we find in Jesus, our Saviour. Men trust in other things—'in reeking tube and iron shard' and sometimes faith looks rather feeble and ordinary in comparison. 'Some trust in chariots and some in horses' (Ps. 20: 7)—in our lifetime it has been trust in the fifteen-inch shell, and lately in the A-bomb or H-bomb—but these things never seem to work out as well as we expected. Before the Second War we read of the wonderful defences the French had built—their Maginot Line, which must surely repel all enemy attacks. We were fascinated by the pictures of these vast defences, and they truly were wonderful, with all kinds of machinery and devices. Parts of them still are. The defences were all right; just one thing was lacking—the human spirit and conviction necessary to use them and defend them! When the time came, the Germans just drove round them. So we come back to our text (Ps. 20: 7): 'Some trust in

horses . . . But *we* will trust in the name of the Lord
our God.'

This is why Paul speaks of 'the God of all comfort', and
Paul knew what he was talking about. His life in Christ
was trials all the way, but his faith remained high. This is
why David says, 'Thy rod and Thy staff, they comfort
me.' The same promise is there for you and me; we can
know this, the supreme comfort, the true comfort.

There is another test of these three levels—how useful
are we to others? Remembering the 'Inasmuch' story, we
can be sure that Jesus is interested in this way of checking
it. It may seem a bit grim to say it, but the world doesn't
want your doubts and fears! The world has enough of its
own! If this deep comfort is yours, by God's grace, you
have something to give the world. Robert Browning spoke
in praise of the man 'who never turned his back, but
marched breast forward; never doubted clouds would
break', and Paul cheered despairing sailors in threatening
seas with his 'Wherefore, sirs; be of good cheer, for I
believe God!' (Acts 27: 25).

'Lord, let me not live to be useless!' was John Wesley's
prayer; and most people do want to be useful to others.
Now, at the first, the armchair level, we are not doing
much for anyone else. Indeed, in the advertisement which
began all this, 'Kenneth' is the opposite of useful. He is
occupying space which father could use, after a long day's
work! At the second, or insurance level, we are at any
rate not a burden to anyone else, and perhaps that is
something! But at the third level! Something different
begins to work. There is something healthy in asking
yourself, 'Have I anything to give the world?' At the very
least it is a splendid change from the oft-heard wail, 'The
world owes me a living!' It doesn't, of course. But the
man who has thankfully accepted Jesus' way of life finds
the courage and the joy of his Lord coming into every-

thing. Jesus knew that His Father *cared*, and His followers today know the same. From the very beginning, something fresh, youthful, and gay came like a breeze into a world that was bored with itself, and it was a fascinating thing.

So here is the true comfort. It comes from the spirit which made the Psalmist say, 'I shall not be moved!' (Psalm 16: 8—and several other places!), but it goes farther than that. It takes a word of Job's (13: 15), 'Though He slay me, yet will I trust in Him'. That word was a tremendous achievement for Job, standing in the darkness with nothing to encourage him except the feeling that God could not be the sort of person that Job's three friends said He was. For the Christian, with all the glad knowledge of what Jesus has done, and the faith that God is like Jesus, this becomes a word of good cheer, of real comfort. If God should bring me even to the door of death, I can gladly believe that there is something better on the other side, and that He leads me on. He is 'the God of all comfort', and our good Lord.

11. *It's a Pity about the Elder Brother*

PEOPLE have always felt that the story of the Prodigal Son (Luke 15) is one of the world's master stories. In this brief space, there seems to be everything—love, greed, adventure, disaster, heart-searching—and then, above all, the happy ending . . . Ah, but does this story end happily? We do think of it in that way. Here is the desperate disillusioned young man in the waste land, bitterly regretting that he ever left the comfort and love of his distant home. But it's too late now; he has made his bed, and he must lie on it . . . *is* it too late? He takes his great decision (perhaps the Authorized Version of the Bible will never be entirely out of date while we can read wonderful sentences like '. . . and when *he came to himself.* . . '. There follows the dull trudge back home. Every familiar sight on the way reminds him of the carefree youth who, a few months before, had come bounding joyously to seek a freedom which too soon became a false dream.

We know this story so well; the father who had never ceased to long for his son's return . . . Was he astonished when at long last he saw the familiar figure plodding along the homeward road? Familiar, but how changed; all the sparkle and the zest gone out of him, walking wearily and rather uncertainly? Probably not. The believer, who in simple trust prays to God for something, is not astonished when it happens. He says, reverently but happily, 'Well, of course! He's like that!' If it doesn't happen he is still content. God knows best. And then came all the joy and the feasting and the dancing. 'And they began to be merry.' Isn't that a fine story? And doesn't it bring cheer to our hearts? Everything is all right again now!

Well—not exactly. He was back home. But this story really ends with the words, 'His elder brother was angry, and would not go in.'

'His elder brother'. Of course; this father had two sons; we read that at the start of the story. Let's confess; we had forgotten the elder brother altogether. We had been so fascinated by the gay, likeable, younger son. In any case, we had had little chance to get to know his elder brother. He was in the fields all day, or sitting up at night with a sick lamb, or going out early to plough or staying out later to get another field in good shape. But this is the story of him as well—and *he would not go in*.

If we think about this story, we can raise a lot of sympathy for the elder brother. Note, to begin with, that *he was in the field*. Not for fun—he was working, and working hard. Work on the farm has never been easy; sometimes, it seems as though Mother Nature is a miser or worse, and grudges the results you are working for. The elder brother was probably cold and certainly tired; he had been doing things that needed to be done. His father relied on him utterly, and, as he got older, was leaving things—leaving everything, perhaps—to him. And so he rather dully 'knocks off', thinks about the wash he'll have, and the meal . . . nothing very special for these next few hours before he tumbles into an early bed, in preparation for a very early start again tomorrow; and perhaps his thoughts turn over some plans for tomorrow's jobs.

But as he gets nearer the farmhouse there is definitely something on—'he heard music and dancing.' You can imagine the noise and the lights, and the very unusual air of it all. As soon as he saw one of the farm hands or an indoor help, he said, 'What's up?'; and a glowing bright face answered, 'Your brother's come home!' Perhaps there was an extra sting for him there, as he realized, quite likely, that his irresponsible young brother had always been the favourite with the servants and the hands. Nobody has ever denied that the elder brother was conscientious and hard-working—and people like that are often not very popular. If the foreman or overseer in a factory insists on having things done properly and finished off he won't be a favourite.

Is this really a happy story? We shall always gladly remember its main message; in fact, that is what we do remember. Anyone can always come back to God as soon as 'he comes to himself'. The only hope for our world is there. But the story really ends with the words, 'He would not go in': and the last thing we see and hear is the father lovingly trying to persuade his elder son to change his mind. There is nothing to tell us that he did.

There is much to be said for the elder brother. His summing up of things in verses 29 and 30 of the Bible chapter was perfectly correct—so far as it went. He *had* worked hard all these years. *He'd* never asked for a fatted calf for a party with his friends—he was too busy to *have* friends! And what he said about his brother was true also. Come to think of it, this story leaves us uncertain about each brother. Did the younger brother really settle down happily at home again? Did he (perhaps the keenest test) give his brother a hand with the hard work of the fields?

There was something about the father, too. You can see from the story that he thought a lot of this elder son, as well he might. He was proud of the way his son had developed and grown; he was his father's right-hand man, and he knew everything about the farm. By now the father relied on him absolutely for everything. 'All that I have is thine!' It was true, and the elder son might have said that himself from a different angle—'Everything you've got I've improved and looked after for you!' Yes; the father thought a lot of his elder son. But . . . had he ever told him so? Or had he somehow taken it for granted! It's so easy to leave it there; the word of thanks, so well deserved, is never spoken—and things would be so much happier if it were.

Yet the elder brother was really farther from home than this younger one had ever been; this impulsive, generous fellow who 'chucked his money about' . . . or his father's! The elder brother would never have wasted all *his* money on riotous living! He'd have seen to it that the other people paid their share of everything, and would have known precisely afterwards how the score had gone! He lacked *love*. For all his good points, there was something more terribly wrong with him than with the younger man. There is altogether more *feeling* about the younger brother, though so far it had led him astray. But we feel that if he *had* spent the weary hours in the fields, it would have been because he loved his father so much. But the elder brother, proud of his ability and of all the work he was doing so well, may have secretly thought of his father as a doddering old fool.

How many times the Bible offers us these choices— Jacob and Esau, Abel and Cain.

The elder son said, 'You never gave *me* a fatted calf!' and the father might have said, 'No—and you've never told me that you love me!' If only the elder son had put aside his very natural and human feelings! If only he had come into the feast and enjoyed his share of it, and then, afterwards, said quietly to his father, 'Well, father; he's been very foolish, but he's come back; that's the main thing. We'll do something with him and for him, you and I together!' Then the father would have loved him utterly, and with a new bond between them they would have gone about the work of the farm, and the task of remaking the lad.

There are people like the elder brother in the world today. They are missing life's deepest secrets and truest

joys. They are good men, upright and exact; but they are
running on a sense of duty. They've never really opened
their hearts to thank God and to love Him for this
wonderful life. Everything the elder brother did was really
done with things that his father had provided (including
his own life!). Men today think and talk in the same way.
The man who says, 'I don't go to church, but I live a
good life', is really putting in a claim to *deserve* all that
God gives without any need to say, 'Thank you' (which
is what *worship* is about). We don't deserve it, and we
can't. It's a free gift. Real life begins when we love God.
If only the love is there the work will follow; we shall
know that our lives are God's and everything in them,
and we shall be delighted to do all we can for His other
children. But it doesn't happen the other way round. If
we work and live without love, we are more likely to
become proud, with the pride that closes the door to real
life. We are as good as anyone else, if not better!

With all his excellences, the elder brother was a little
man; the younger had in him something that could make
him great: and let us hope that that was the way it went.
If only, in this wonderful story, the young man really
learns his lesson from what has happened, and accepts the
challenge of the second chance, he will be a greater man
than ever the elder brother could be (unless *he* learns the
way to love).

Let us look into our own hearts. How are we thinking
of life and of God and of ourselves? There is only one
real way. We must be as loving, as generous, as the
younger brother, as keen on adventure and life; *and* we
must be as laborious and as dutiful as the elder brother.

But we must start with the love! It was when the first
handful of Christians 'were all together in one place'
(Acts 2: 1) that they received the great revelation of God's
Spirit which we call Pentecost or Whitsun. Our church

services and meetings today are just for that; we can learn to taste the love that God gives, to share what He is giving us and to take our part of what He is giving to others. In that sentence we have described *fellowship*: and in fellowship people *grow*. The expectant Christians before Pentecost loved Jesus, loved God, and loved each other. So they were ready for the next great step. Love opens the doors; self-righteousness or hate closes them, and we get no farther. There are men and women who will never understand life, or really live, until they open their hearts in the love that looks outward to other people.

This wonderful story of the Prodigal Son is all the more wonderful because it has its light and dark, its gay and grim notes, all blended together. Some of us have very good reasons for letting our thoughts dwell on the elder brother. We rather feel that we are like him in some ways; we can tackle a job with energy and do it quickly and well; and we can't help knowing that it is better done than when some people do it! But we are very much afraid that we may share, too, his lovelessness and the greyness of his outlook. So we come to the good Father in prayer and humbleness, asking Him to confirm and strengthen and increase anything that is good about us, but (above all) to take lovelessness and pride away and plant within us the love that can do all things.

12. *John did no Miracles ...*

Supposing you went to a concert one night—at your church, or somewhere in the town; and supposing that when you opened the programme to see what was going to happen, you read, all set out in neat lines, something like this:

'Tom Morris is quite unable to play the piano.
It would be perfectly awful if Hilda Russell tried
     to sing to you.
Mary Jones has absolutely no memory for recitations.
David Brown is a complete fiasco at conjuring.'

... you would be a bit surprised.
But if the programme read:

'Tom Morris	Conjurer
Hilda Russell	Piano Solo
Mary Jones	Contralto
David Brown	Elocution'

you would sit back in pleasant anticipation!

Here are three things that are true:

Everybody can do *something*.
The best thing is to concentrate on *that*.
It is wise not to worry about the things we can't do.

Three things: and God helps us each time.
'Concentrate on what you can do' (the second of these) and 'Don't worry about what you *can't* do!' (the third) are much easier when God is helping you; and perhaps the first ('Everybody can do something') is never so true as when God is there.

John—John the Baptist, that is—did no miracles. Now, that was a pity. He had something to tell people, and in those days there was nothing like a few striking miracles to make people run together, to look and listen. Science (in the way we talk about it) had hardly been born, and most people felt that gods and mysterious beings were very close, and able to do all kinds of strange things. People rushed together when Jesus worked a miracle, though He didn't work miracles for that reason, and you can see in the Bible that Jesus often felt that the miracles got in His way. He did something wonderful to help some poor soul, and wanted to leave it there, but people stood and talked about it, instead of seeing the wonderful meaning behind it all. But John did nothing like this.

Fortunately, the sentence doesn't end there. It goes on '. . . but all things that John spake of this man were true' (John 10: 41). That was a grateful word. It pays John a very fine compliment. John had pointed people to Jesus, and of course they had not been disappointed. They had come to feel that there was more in life now. They remembered, too, the man who had shown them the way. John's Gospel has a similar word earlier on, as well (1: 37), 'The two disciples heard *him* (John) speak, and they followed *Jesus*.' Any preacher, or any Christian, should be happy if people could write that about him.

First, then, *everybody can do something.* Do you believe that? It's true, though in some people discouragement or perhaps failure has crushed it down. That's where God comes in, and we shall think about that later. Everybody can do something. It's a very cheering thing to believe. Perhaps it is only to smile, to write a letter, saying a word of appreciation or encouragement; but what a difference that might make to someone who is nervous or lonely! Everybody can do something. Let's stress what we *can* do. Let's try to be positive about ourselves. Then we may see more of our opportunities. What can we do? Here is a very comforting thought to start with; we can never be blamed, not in any reasonable way, for not doing something that is absolutely beyond us! John the Baptist would never lie under condemnation; miracles were not his job. His one job was to point to Jesus: to be a voice, the first voice that had prophesied for hundreds of years—and this was why the Jews had been so thrilled when he suddenly appeared, as Elijah and Amos had done before him.

We may often wish that we could do other things. Perhaps there were times when John wished that he could work miracles. It might have helped his effectiveness, too; people might have listened more. But this was not his job. And his job had to be done, and he was the man to do it. I like the story of the boy working in a City office. They asked him what he did, and he said, 'I'm a doer!' This puzzled them, and he explained. 'Well,' he said, 'the boss tells the chief clerk, and the chief clerk tells Mr .... and he tells ....' and so the boy went on, until he said '. . . and Mr .... tells me; and I've got no one to tell, so I do it!' It looks as though it was as well to have the *boy* there, anyway!

The actor who can play the clown splendidly, quite often wants to be the hero! These things are natural, but we are really better doing our own job.

In days now almost entirely gone by, many countrymen had to do with horses. What a bond used to grow between the man and his horses! He knew just what each horse could do. 'Blossom' would carry a heavy load splendidly, but only for a short distance. 'Fairy' would last the whole day, whatever he gave her to do. They didn't stress what 'Fairy' and 'Blossom' *couldn't* do; and they didn't grumble at them for not doing what was not in their nature and their make-up. They built the day's work round what

each would and could do. (Here is a whole world that has
vanished now that the lorry is seen—and heard and smelt
—everywhere!) A man whose job it is to write plays, does
much the same thing. Gilbert and Sullivan wrote comic
operas, as many of you know, and by the time Gilbert had
written the words for three or four operas, he was really
writing his plots and words around the actors and actresses
who were to play the parts. He knew them by then, and
would think, 'That will be just the line for So-and-so!'
In many a factory or office (in small businesses, at any
rate) the head of the firm may know very well what the
people can do best. It's not much good asking for *this*,
but he or she will do *that* very well.

It is true, of course, that until now in the world's history
millions of people have never had a chance to do or be
what they were really fitted for. There must have been
many 'mute inglorious Miltons' who might have done
wonders if they had had the chance. God has honoured
the courage of people like that, who have quietly done
what they had to do, to His glory, without complaining.
Another thing that is true: what looks like 'contentment'
in some people is really a sort of fear of new things—or
even a sort of laziness. If the chance comes to us to follow
some new way that does really call to something inside us,
this we should certainly do. But all this will be through
God's special guidance, and we can leave this to
Him.

For the rest, then, let your mind and interest bear on the
job that you *can* do. Maybe that job isn't what you wanted;
it's not what you hoped for when you were young and
dreamed your dreams. Many of us were going to do such
great things; but it hasn't worked out like that. Yet there
can be a lot of satisfaction in doing what we can do.
Daniel March's fine hymn ('Hark! the voice of Jesus
saying') has point here:

If you cannot cross the ocean,
  And the heathen lands explore,
 You can find the heathen nearer,
   You can help them at your door;

That word just now about 'mute inglorious Miltons'—
Milton himself might have been like that. John Milton
was a great writer of books and pamphlets. It got so that
the Government of the day trembled under his words.
But few people today know about them. One of his most
famous writings is called . . . *steady!* . . . his *A-re-o-pag-i-
ti-ca*, which is a great defence of liberty. But if you were
asked what John Milton did, you would almost certainly
say, 'He wrote *Paradise Lost*': and you might also remember
his *Paradise Regained*. Now, these great works came after
the awful blow of his blindness. People must have said,
'*That's* finished him!'—and some of them not too sorry
about it, either. But he had learned much, and done much,
when he wrote, 'They also serve who only stand and wait.'

Sir Arthur Pearson went blind in later days; but a whole
generation is grateful to him for all that St Dunstan's has
come to stand for. Daniel was taken from his own country
as a lad; surely the end of all things, but in the foreign
land he became the king's prime minister. And look at
Joseph. Even if one has a sneaking human feeling that
Joseph got what he asked for, we can praise him for the
wonderful way in which, with God's help, he turned the
disaster to good. 'Ye meant evil against me,' he said later
on to his brothers, 'but God meant it for good' (Gen.
50: 20). Yet who would have blamed Joseph if he had
thrown up the sponge and had just disappeared from the
story—a nameless slave in Egypt? The young Dr Barnardo
may have looked forward to a distinguished career as a
specialist; but when he saw the boys sleeping rough in
London Docks he answered the call for which we remember

him today. (Few would have remembered him now if he *had* become a distinguished specialist!) And in 1738 a conscientious and gifted young Oxford professor came back from America in sore distress. 'I went to convert the Indians,' said John Wesley, 'but, O, who will convert me?' His only hope seemed to be to go back to Oxford and teach once more. When his friend, George Whitefield, invited him to preach to the colliers of Kingswood, he went without realizing that this was going to lead him to his life work.

Whatever we might have been, or longed to be, here is something that we can be for Him; and perhaps this is just the thing He wants, even if it is not what we hoped for. And remember that Jesus 'keeps it ordinary'—His promise is that if we give a cup of cold water to someone who is thirsty, there is a quality about this that will last for ever. That is a very ordinary thing; but perhaps it is ordinary things that really help people.

Now, if we could not have said at every turn, 'God helps here—and here!' all these things would have sounded pretty ineffective. 'Pull yourself together!' men will say. Sometimes that can work wonders—but there are times when we don't seem able to respond to friendly advice like that. We know a lot of people who just can't cope with things. They often know what they ought to do, but the power . . . Ah! that is the word. There is a promise about power; and it is for everyone. 'He giveth power to the faint' (Is. 40: 29). He gives vision, too. God can come into our lives and show us far horizons, wonderful opportunities, at home, where we work, in the places we were finding so narrow and dull. It's like looking at a leaf or at a snowflake, or a bee's wing, and finding these ordinary enough. But a scientist lets you look at these things through his microscope, and what you see just amazes you. Or you see a faint blur in the dark sky; a telescope would show you glories that would give you fresh reasons for worshipping their great Maker. Discoveries like these are just as real in the world of human life.

People said, 'John worked no miracles!' and that was true. John wasn't that sort of man, and he had to face it, and they had to face it. But later on they were saying something more—something that mattered—'. . . but all the things that John spake of this man were true!', and they added, '. . . and aren't we glad that he said them!' This is what John was *for*, and it was what John did. Jesus gave him the same rank as the great and famous Elijah; he was the voice of God.

So here is the challenge for us all. This is something that each of us can do. It may not be what we thought of doing or wanted to do; but it looks as though it is what God wants. Every man has something he can do—let us do it. Men may come to say of you, as they said of John: 'Well, he doesn't look much, and (. . . this and that . . . !) . . . but—he did do this, and how glad we are that he did!'

13. *He Painted the Walls of his Prison*

THOMAS GIRTIN was born with the desire to paint. That was in 1775; he lived but twenty-seven years, and it was Turner himself who said later, 'Had Tom Girtin lived, I should have starved!' That was rather flattering, and Girtin is generally counted as a pleasant painter of only average ability. But you can see some very nice pictures of his in the galleries.

When he was quite young he was apprenticed to Edward Dayes, a leading artist of the time.

Jealousy is not our main subject here, but there is plenty of jealousy in this story, and it is worth remembering what a terrible thing jealousy is—and, to be honest, how very natural it is to human beings until God helps us to be bigger. When Saul's troops returned from battle in Israel of old, and the women greeted their return, they sang, 'Saul has slain his thousands, and David his ten thousands' (1 Sam. 18: 7), and we read, 'Saul eyed David from that time and forward.' We are not surprised!

Turning back to Dayes and Girtin, we can sympathize with the older man. It must be a galling thing to realize, perhaps slowly, when you have started someone on his way, shown him the very beginnings of the job, that he is going to be better at it than you are yourself. You had your dreams, and things have not gone as you hoped. You are *not* going to reach the top of the tree. Then this stripling comes along, all unconscious that there is great-ness in him; clumsy, and yet already there are hints of something wonderful. This is what Dayes saw. Girtin did it awkwardly at first, of course, and the next moment he was doing something coarse or ugly in outline and colour. But, now and again, there were things about young Girtin that took Dayes's breath away. '*I* couldn't do that!' he confessed to himself. He was in the presence of greatness. Perhaps he was right; Girtin's pathetic twenty-seven years of life gave him little chance to show. Dayes was saying to himself, 'They will remember this man when my name is forgotten.' That, of course, did turn out to be true. Perhaps we can sympathize with Dayes.

But that is not how the great man behaves. We see the proper way in John the Baptist, in his ungrudging honesty and realism. What a sensation John the Baptist had made! The first prophet for hundreds of years! As men had read their Bibles (the Old Testament, that is) the words of Jeremiah and Isaiah, Amos and Hosea, had echoed in their hearts. These men had stood for God and righteousness, and had stood in the way of kings when it was needful. For years before John the Baptist, people had been hoping for another prophet, and then John came! He brooded in the wilderness and then started his preaching with such power that everyone flocked to hear him. But when, one day, there came with the crowds a young man who wanted to be baptized like the rest, he knew who He was; and the days and weeks that followed made it clear that Jesus was the rising star, and that John's star was setting. But John was wonderfully loyal to what God had told him, and he said simply, 'He must increase, and I must decrease.' It wants a lot of saying, but John said it. Dayes, watching the young man Girtin, didn't say it, and couldn't say it. He showed his jealousy in other ways, too. Instead of teaching Girtin and watching over his progress, he used him for all the 'dirty jobs': things that could teach him nothing. He kept him for weeks and months filling in the colours on prints—not much different from what little children do with their painting books, though (of course) needing to be done carefully and properly.

One day, something really snapped in young Girtin's

mind, and he said, 'I won't do it!' and pushed the prints aside. Nothing better for the jealous Dayes. He stood on his rights as the master of an apprentice and Girtin was taken off to prison, and prison in those days was something cruel and hopeless. Girtin was in prison; and in prison he would stay.

There he did stay, too. But one day the Earl of Essex came to see the prison, because he sympathized with the hopeless people there. They took him from cell to cell, noisome and foul, and he saw prisoner after prisoner, sitting in a corner, hopeless and sunk in despair. Then the turnkey opened another door; it was Girtin's cell this time.

The first thing that the Earl saw was not the prisoner, but the pictures on the walls of the cell. The walls were covered with beautiful pictures. We don't know how Girtin had got his paints and his brushes, but there it was. The walls glowed with his work. The Earl was surprised, interested, and pleased. What a contrast with the other cells he had seen! Instead of a cowering, desperate figure, here was a young man, naturally pale, and none the better for his confinement, but still eager to express his gifts as best he could. The Earl enquired about Girtin, and he was soon released. Unfortunately, as we have seen, he did not live many years, but he progressed steadily towards the honoured place which he holds in the realm of painting.

'Stone walls do not a prison make.' Well, they do, and they can be very irksome. But they cannot confine the spirit that soars above them, and Girtin showed what was in him, even there.

When a Church of England priest, the first Bishop of New Zealand, went there in 1841 to preach to the Maoris, they took this eager young man and imprisoned him in a sty. That was a fine ending to the dreams with which he had crossed half the world! Or at least a sad interruption, and he must have been dispirited. A bit later the Maoris peeped in to see what their prisoner was doing, and they found that he had gathered together all sorts of bits of rubbish, odd wood and so on, and he had piled them up in the shape of an altar. There he was, worshipping his God. The Maoris took him out of the pigsty, for, as they said to one another, 'What can you do with a man like that?' His courage in such a situation impressed them strongly; his zeal and Gospel power later convinced them, and Selwyn became the first Bishop of New Zealand.

There have been others like him. It was in a sick room that Anne Brontë and Frances Ridley Havergal wrote hymns that help our faith today; and they all face us with the glorious fact that a man or woman in a small or difficult place can, with God's help, make something wonderful of it.

We have been thinking of people who made something big out of something small, because they had the will to win through. But what about the opposite? Some people, given big opportunities, big gifts to start with, turn them into something small—fritter away wonderful things and waste them. Which are we? What are we doing with what we have? Leave aside for the moment the fact that other people did get a better start than we got; the important thing is always 'What are we doing with what we have?' *Are we painting the walls?* A man may complain that his life is a prison, and he may seem to have every right to complain, and be entitled to a lot of sympathy. It is a pity that he wasn't given a better start. But is he painting the walls? If he is not—honestly, is he showing himself *worthy* of something better? When films and novels always had happy endings, you could see or read a romantic story where the boss of a firm noted a lad doing well, and promoted him—and usually he ended up by marrying the

boss's daughter! You may have smiled and dismissed it all
as imaginary, and too good to be true. But wait a moment:
perhaps that sort of thing doesn't often happen. But even
less often does the boss see a slacker, a sulker, an idler,
and promote *him*! The one may not often happen; the
other never will!

You have talents, you feel, that entitle you to a better
show in life? Well: start by proving it! If you feel that
you are in prison, paint the walls! Make this grim, un-
promising situation brighter by bringing faith and hope
and love to it! When, in the Parable of the Talents, the
master came round, he praised the two-talented man with
exactly the same praise that he had used for the five-
talented man. The five-talented man made another five;
but the two-talented man made another two, and that is
the same percentage!

As always, our Saviour is our best example. Born in
the hovel attached to an inn, because there was no room
anywhere else; born into a very ordinary family where (it
seems) father died early on, and the eldest son would have
to take over and keep the family—what scope was there
for one so wonderful as Jesus? Yet we believe that even
in the village Jesus lived perfectly the life which (at that
time) was His to live. Some of our gifted writers have
imagined that when Jesus made a yoke, a chair, or whatever, it was perfectly made. His task was to be the village
carpenter, and He did this perfectly, with all the little
bodging jobs that people took to him.

> *And so the Word had breath, and wrought*
> *With human hands the creed of creeds,*
> *In loveliness of perfect deeds,*
> *More strong than all poetic thought.*

We are thinking about inequalities and about chances

great and small, and it will be useful if we determine to do all we can to make our world a better place, so that all may start with a good chance. The child born into the poor home, the broken and quarrelling home, the criminal home, does seem to have fewer chances than the child born into the good home. Yet we read of so many men and women who started with nothing, but who won through, that clearly it is not only our circumstances that count, but ourselves as well. Over all the circumstances of this strange life is God, and His promises and His power are there for everyone. There is 'grace for every need': so that if a life seems to have extra difficulties, there is extra grace.

Which kind are we, then? The kind that spoils the opportunities that are there, the kind that turns great things into small ones by wasting them and just being 'fed up'? Or the other kind? Am I painting the walls of my prison, and making the best of what I have, so that I am fitting myself for something better?

The Earl of Essex may be long in coming; there were surely many weary months for young Girtin, and no prospect of anything ever happening, before the door opened to admit his deliverer. But to all men who wait in hope, the King comes at last. 'Well done, good and faithful servant,' He says. And then we are glad that we did keep the faith. It would have been easy to complain and be cynical as other people have.

In Girtin's story it was what the Earl thought that counted, not the jealous spite of Dayes. In all life it is God's view that matters. The missionary may die in the distant land without honour or remembrance; many a quiet man may be ignored and disregarded, and never honoured as he deserves to be. But there is an everlasting record which is called 'The Lamb's Book of Life', and their names are written there—for always.

I will paint the walls of my prison. The painting itself will give me some happiness, some uprising of spirit. And in the end it will lead me into more spacious, lovelier places, and I shall see the King in His beauty, because, in His unseen strength, I have kept the faith.

14. *I was a Stranger*

In the olden days most people lived and died in the place where they had been born. Everyone knew everyone else, and that has its points, as village people know today. You can't *pretend* very much in a place where you have all lived together for years. In other ways it could be deadening, of course, and that is why there were always a few bold spirits who went off to try their fortune, sometimes right round the world. We are now being told that the bold Norsemen had crossed the ocean in their small boats and discovered America long before Christopher Columbus, and there are wonderful stories of early explorers on romantic journeys—Marco Polo, who started from Italy and got to China, and Sir Francis Drake who is famous for the first journey right round the world—the first we know of, at any rate.

Nowadays, nearly everyone is on the move, and journeys to other lands become a commonplace for many. Trains and ships and planes are crowded, and cars cross the world. Our young people visit other countries from a very early age; and this is all to the good. The more the peoples of every land get to know one another, the better chance there is of world friendship.

In the old days people worked where they were born. For a long time now, men and women have flocked to places where they could find work, especially better-paid work—to Manchester and Birmingham for a very long time; to Coventry and Dagenham more recently. After the first war, the Government established places like the Slough Trading Estate, and people came from every part of the land. You could hear every dialect of the country along the streets of new houses that they built. Nowadays, people's jobs are moved. A great company decides that it will do better by shifting its factory to another part of the country, or one firm 'takes over' another; sometimes, too, the Government persuades a business to move to a part of the land where there is no work, and certainly the Government is doing this with its own departments. Then, too, there are the 'new towns' created to relieve pressure on the old ones—the people who join these are often called by the unflattering title of 'overspill'! When the clever people and the government officials talk about all this, they cover it under the neat phrase 'the mobility of labour', but it isn't as neat as that for the countless families that have to leave their houses and homes, their churches, clubs, and friends, and that one day find themselves in a new place altogether. Even if a man, or a man and his family, does decide to do all this voluntarily, it takes away a lot of life's comforts and pleasures for a time. When it is done over your head, and suddenly, it must be very hard to bear.

When these things do happen, there are wonderful opportunities for the churches. True, we are apt to say sometimes that these people are 'not the church type', and on the human level it can look a bit like that. Many of the new people look eagerly in their new districts for fried fish shops and Bingo halls, not churches. But it is wonderful what churches can do where there is a sincere spirit of friendship. Certainly there are some wonderful churches in new areas. One real advantage in a brand-new church is that if everyone *is* new together, there is a fine chance to work out new things. No one can say, 'We've always done it like *this*!', because until very recently no one has done it at all! In this new church everyone is growing up together.

Someone has said that if our churches did nothing more than lead to the making of friendships and do away with

loneliness, they would still do a wonderful job! We can
see what he meant, though friendships need something to
keep them alive, and to keep them constant, and the deep
things of church life must be there. But friendships can be
a blessing at such a time. It isn't nice being a stranger.
You don't know where things are in the new place; you
don't know where the roads turn off, and where the buses
run, and where the shops are that sell the things you like.
Your old butcher knew your particular cut, and your
confectioner used to push the toffee across the counter
without your asking for it; the newsboy knew which of
the evening papers you wanted, and so on.

When God called Jeremiah to work for him as a prophet,
Jeremiah tried to tell God just how awkward and unfitted
he felt for the work. What he actually said was, 'I am like
a little child; I know not how to go out or to come in',
and that is a good way of describing the life in a new
place. Everything is awkward and unknown; and most of
us hate the unknown.

In passing (for it is not our main subject at present),
it is a truly blessed task to make strangers feel at home.
'A stranger shalt thou not wrong; for ye were strangers
in the land of Egypt' (Ex. 22: 21—repeated four times in
later scriptures, to show that it was *meant*!). And Jesus
says, in the 'Inasmuch' story (Matthew 25), 'I was a
stranger, and ye took Me in.'

There must be thousands of people who have heard of
Paul, who have never heard of Barnabas. Yet without
Barnabas there might never have been a *Saint* Paul. Ask
yourself; if you had lived in Jerusalem in those days, and
the man called Paul had come to your church and said,
'I'm a Christian now!', would you have believed him?
The last time you had seen this man, he was the killer
of the Christians. Perhaps he had caused the death of
some brother, or sister, or great friend of yours. They

might have looked very coldly on Paul—there have always been 'fifth-columnists': it was only the *name* that was new in the Second War. Was it possible that, despite all the golden opinions Paul had brought with him from Damascus, this man was seeking to worm his way in and then betray them all from the inside?

Things might have gone very wrong but for Barnabas, with his ready smile and his encouragement. The stranger was taken right into their hearts, and the great Apostle started his wonderful work.

Well: for some of us the memory of being a stranger is a very clear one. We were new and needed to watch everything, to test and try everything. It was all very tense and uncertain; we knew that something would go wrong if we were not very careful; indeed, it often did go wrong, even when we *were* careful.

Now we are getting close to our real subject. Many people are strangers to God. They don't deny that there is one, just as they don't deny that they have neighbours. But they don't *know* Him. Some of them wish they might know Him, but they don't. Some people don't even want to know God. God stands for things that are right outside their lives. Some of them have indeed realized pretty clearly that if God is real, and if they did make room for Him in their lives, they would have to get rid of a lot of things they value and like. So they take good care not to think about Him at all.

Now, some people don't want to know their neighbours. They resist every effort you make even to pass the time of day with them. This is their way of living, and they have every right to live like that if they want to, even if it seems a bit unfriendly. God is not content to leave things like that. God, in Charles Wesley's wonderful word, '*begs* us to be friends'. That is a very surprising word, if you follow it through, though Charles Wesley is absolutely right. You may hear or see, by means of radio or TV, programmes telling about our wonderful world, or the children may bring home such things from school. Such a marvellous creation tells us much about a marvellous Creator. But for the Christian, God is not, first of all, a great technician or the great organizer. However much we marvel at what men tell us about His work, He is our Father. And with His great heart of love, God wants to know you and me. His 'great idea' in making all His worlds was so that He could enjoy for ever (in what we usually call 'Heaven') the closest friendship with all the children He has made. This is why He died on the Cross, and this was the only way to bring us back. God can't bear His children to be strangers to Him. Christ died for us—for each one of us.

When you see a doctor you have known and trusted for years, it feels as though he is giving all his time and care to *you*. You haven't got to rush; you can take your time. You know very well that he has crowds of other patients— you had to wait outside for a lot of them to go in and come away before you could get in here, and when it was your turn you left a crowd in the waiting room. But this bit of time is yours; he doesn't seem to hurry (though he won't waste time either!). It's the same when you really get into touch with God, and the wisest of God's saints, the most brilliant theological scholar, will often be a man who finds the words, 'A little talk with Jesus makes it right, all right!', a real picture of the Christian life.

It's lovely to be where you are at home. You may go for a holiday abroad and enjoy it; but it's nice to get back and have some real money in your purse, and to find the traffic on the proper side of the road, and the buses the right colour! It's lovely to be at home with God, too. 'Ye are no more strangers,' says Paul in Eph. 2: 19. This is a wonderful thought. We can be ourselves at home;

indeed, we can't be anything else, and that is absolutely restful. You don't pretend anything at home; it wouldn't be any good, for they all know you for what you are! We take our coats off and sit in our shirtsleeves; we put our slippers on; we are truly at ease. God's welcome is the same. He loves us—but He 'weighs us up'! God welcomes us; He understands; He will encourage us—or, where we need it, tell us where we are wrong.

Don't be a 'stranger' with God. He has come more than halfway to meet you. Bible students saw long ago that the beautiful story of the Prodigal Son is only half Christian. It's a wonderful story, with the picture of the father waiting at the door, or perhaps going down the pathway towards the road. But the story Jesus *lived* shows the Heavenly Father going the whole way, right to the lost country. His children were truly lost, but the Father went and found them. Remember His promise to each one of us. 'Behold, I stand at the door and knock: if any man hear my voice and open the door, I will come in to him' (Rev. 3: 20).

> *Mercy He doth for thousands keep;*
> *He goes and seeks the one lost sheep,*
> *And brings His wanderer home;*
> *And every soul that sheep might be;*
> *Come then, my Lord, and gather me,*
> *My Jesus, quickly come!*